The **Sikh** Experience

Seeking **religion**

Jan Thompson

Foundation

Hodder Murray
A MEMBER OF THE HODDER HEADLINE GROUP

Acknowledgements

Dedicated to:
Anita Compton, a friend and colleague.

Notes:

CE = Common Era.
BCE = Before the Common Era.
CE corresponds to AD, and BCE corresponds to BC. The years are the same, but CE and BCE can be used by anyone regardless of their religion. (AD and BC are Christian: AD stands for Anno Domini – in the Year of Our Lord, i.e. Jesus Christ; BC stands for Before Christ.)

Key words are explained in the Glossary on page 63

Orders: please contact Bookpoint Ltd, 130 Milton Park, Abingdon, Oxon OX14 4SB. Telephone: (44) 01235 827720, Fax: (44) 01235 400454. Lines are open from 9.00–6.00, Monday to Saturday, with a 24 hour message answering service.

You can also order through our website www.hoddereducation.co.uk

British Library Cataloguing in Publication Data
A catalogue record for this title is available from The British Library

ISBN-10: 0 340 77584 X
ISBN-13: 978 0 340 77584 4

Impression number 10 9 8 7 6 5
Year 2005

Cover photo from Corbis
All illustrations supplied by Daedalus with special thanks to John McIntyre.
Typeset by Wearset, Boldon, Tyne and Wear.
Printed for Hodder Murray, an imprint of Hodder Education,
a member of the Hodder Headline Group, 338 Euston Road, London NW1 3BH.

The publisher would like to thank the following for permission to reproduce copyright photographs in this book:

J Allan Cash Photolibrary: p43t; Hulton Getty Picture Collection Ltd: p51; David Rose: p27; Malkit Singh: p59.

All remaining photographs courtesy of Philip Emmett.

The author would like to thank Harjinder Boparai at HSB Productions Ltd for permission to reproduce the quotation on page 59.

Minor adaptations have been made to some quotations to render them more accessible to the readership.

Every effort has been made to contact the holders of copyright material but if any have been inadvertently overlooked, the publisher will be pleased to make the necessary alterations at the first opportunity

Contents

1 Guru Nanak

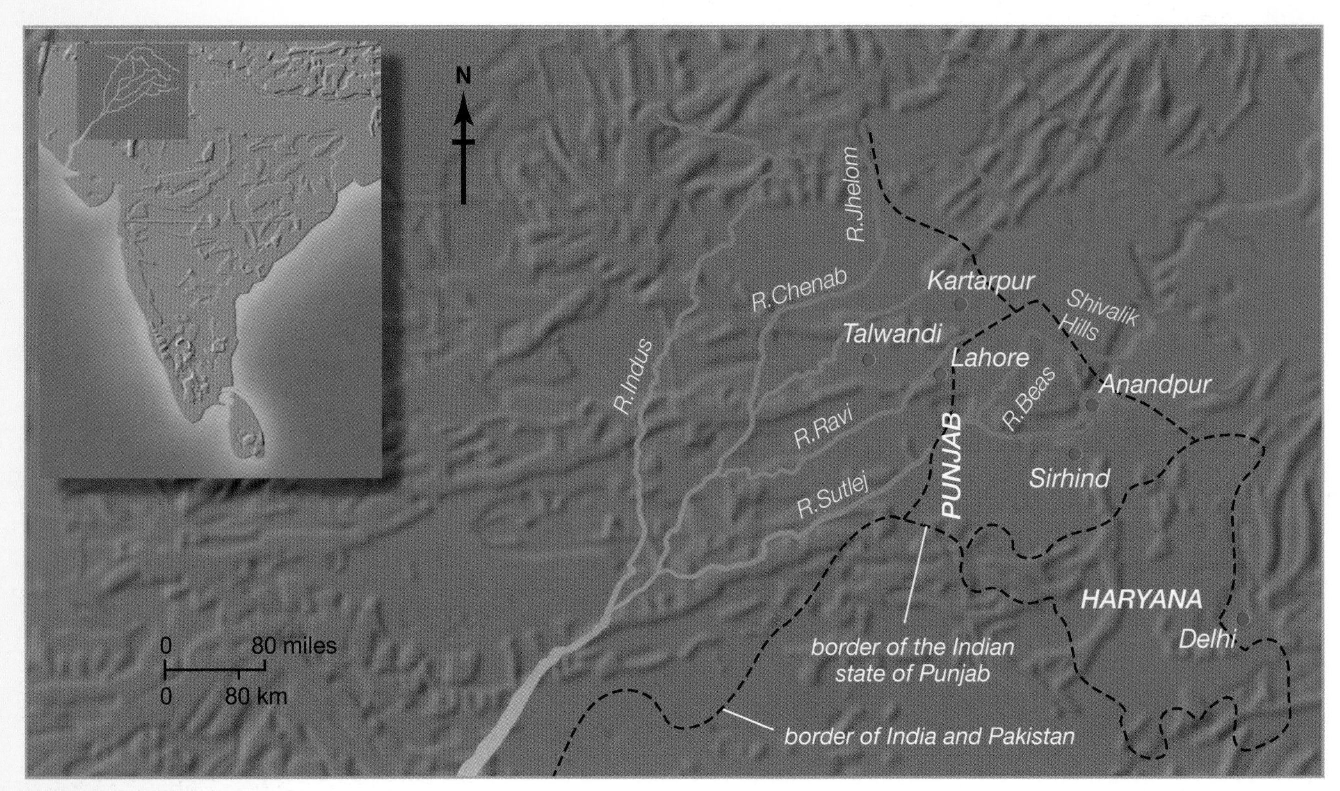

▲ *Map of the Punjab*

Look at the map above. It shows the Punjab, sitting between India and Pakistan. The Punjab is named after the '5' rivers that flow through the land. ('Punj' means 'five'.) Can you trace them with your finger on the map?

The Punjab is where Guru Nanak was born. He started the Sikh religion. **Most Sikhs still live in the Punjab.** Find Talwandi on the map. This is where he was born.

Guru Nanak lived from 1469 to 1539 CE. This was about 500 years ago. That may seem a long time ago to you, but it means that Sikhism is the youngest of the 6 main world religions.

'Guru' is not Nanak's name. It is a title. It is an Indian word which means 'Teacher'.

> It is through actions that some come nearer to God and some wander away.
>
> *Guru Nanak*

Key words

Sikhism
guru
miracle

▲ *Guru Nanak*

There are stories about Nanak as a boy which show how special he was. Some of them are miracles:

- The stories tell how he amazed religious teachers with his wisdom.
- They tell of his love of the poor. On one occasion, his father gave him some money to use for trade. But Nanak gave it away!
- One story tells how a deadly cobra shaded him from the sun while he slept.
- Another story tells how he let cattle go into someone's field and eat the crop. The owner of the field was very angry. But when they looked, the cattle had done no harm.

  Nanak did not draw attention to his miracles. He knew that any power he had came from God:

> Mighty is the Lord, and great His gifts.
>
> *Guru Nanak*

In those days, people got married at an early age. Nanak was about 16 when he married. They had 2 sons. He worked as an accountant until he was about 30. He was known for his honesty.

He was not very interested in work. He spent time in prayer and helping people, especially the poor and lowly:

> Lord, your love falls on the land, and the lowly are cared for.
>
> *Guru Nanak*

One day, he was bathing in the river when something very strange happened. He said that he met God. He returned 3 days later to begin his religious work.

It's a sign! He's going to be a great teacher.

▲ *Stories from his early life*

1 What is the name of the land where Sikhism began?

2 What does 'guru' mean?

3 Discuss: what is a miracle? Which of the stories about Nanak are miracles?

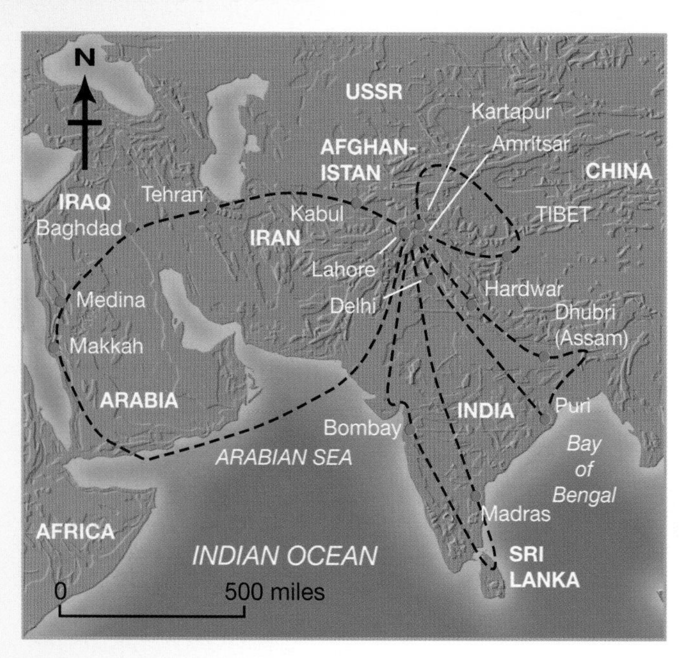

▲ *The places Guru Nanak visited*

Guru Nanak went on 4 long journeys. He taught people wherever he went. The map shows that he travelled from one end of India to the other. He also travelled to Arabia, and to the holy places of Islam.

His friend, Mardana, travelled with him. He was a musician. Guru Nanak made up poems, and Mardana put them to music. This helped people to remember them.

> Whose path shall I follow? I shall follow God's path. God is neither Hindu nor Muslim and the path which I follow is God's.
>
> *Guru Nanak*

Most Indians belonged to the religions of Hinduism or Islam. Nanak was brought up as a Hindu. But he refused to choose one religion.

▼ *Some of the things Guru Nanak did on his journeys*

Guru Nanak started a new town called Kartarpur. This means 'the seat of God'. Can you find it on the first map? It was where his followers could live. They could work and pray together. He called his followers Sikhs. This means 'disciples'. A disciple is someone who learns.

Guru Nanak finished his travels and lived at Kartarpur. He opened a free kitchen there. Meals were served to visitors. Everyone ate together because all Sikhs are equal.

Guru Nanak died on 22 September 1539 CE. One of his disciples, Lehna, became the next Guru.

▲ *How Lehna was chosen to be the next Guru*

1 In pairs, look at the pictures of what Guru Nanak did on his travels. Write down TWO messages he taught.

2 Still in pairs, look at the pictures on this page. Explain why Guru Nanak chose Lehna to be the next Sikh leader rather than his own sons.

3 Sharing food with someone is a sign of friendship.

a) If you went out for a special meal (perhaps for your birthday), who would you invite?

b) Why should Sikhs eat together, whether they are rich or poor?

2 After Guru Nanak

There were 10 human leaders of Sikhism. Guru Nanak was the first. He chose Lehna to be the next Guru. Lehna was humble and willing to work hard for Sikhism.

> **TASK**
> Do you think humbleness and hard work are good qualities for a leader? What other qualities are important for a leader?

2 Guru Angad (1504–1552 CE)

Nanak gave Lehna a new name. He called him Angad. This meant 'part of myself'. It showed that he would carry on Nanak's work. Guru Angad was a good man. He did many things to help Sikhism grow. He

- set up schools for young Sikhs;
- encouraged Sikhs to keep fit;
- developed the free kitchen;
- collected and wrote down the hymns of Guru Nanak;
- made up many hymns of his own.

3 Guru Amar Das (1479–1574 CE)

Guru Angad chose Guru Amar Das to be the third leader of Sikhism. When the emperor visited the new Guru, he was asked to sit on the floor with everyone else. He

- organised the Sikhs into 22 districts;
- wrote the Anand Sahib. This is a prayer said near the end of every Sikh service of worship.

▶ *Guru Amar Das, the third guru*

4 Guru Ram Das (1534–1581 CE)

He was the son-in-law of the third Guru. His name meant 'servant of God'. He

- sent out Sikhs far and wide to teach this religion;
- bought some land for a Sikh city. He built a large pool there. It was to become the centre of Sikhism.

◄ *The city that Guru Ram Das started. It is called Amritsar – 'pool of nectar'. The Golden Temple is in the middle of the pool*

5 Guru Arjan Dev (1563–1606 CE)

He was the youngest son of Guru Ram Das. He

- finished the pool that his father had started;
- built the Golden Temple in the centre of the pool;
- put together the first Sikh holy book. It was called the Adi Granth;
- opened a centre for lepers.

The new emperor tried to stamp out Sikhism. Guru Arjan Dev died for his faith. He was roasted alive and his body was thrown in the river.

▲ *An early hand-written copy of the Adi Granth*

6 Guru Hargobind (1595–1644 CE)

He was Guru Arjan Dev's only child. He

- trained the Sikhs to fight to defend themselves;
- built a fort at Amritsar.

There were many battles with the emperor's army. He was put in prison for a time. Every year Sikhs celebrate the time when he was freed at the festival of Divali.

7 Guru Har Rai

(1630–1661 CE)

He was the grandson of the sixth Guru. He tried to live in peace and spread Sikhism.

8 Guru Har Krishan

(1626–1664 CE)

He was the second son of the seventh Guru. He was only 5 years old when he became Guru. He looked after people who were ill with smallpox. Sadly, he caught the disease himself and died. He was the only Guru who was not married with a family.

9 Guru Tegh Bahadur

(1621–1675 CE)

He was the fifth son of Guru Hargobind. His name meant 'brave sword'. He died a martyr. This is how it happened:

The emperor was Muslim and wanted everyone to become Muslims. He was going to kill the Hindu priests. They went to this Guru for help. He told them to tell the emperor that they would change their beliefs if the Guru could be converted to Islam. The Guru could not be converted. He was beheaded when he refused to become a Muslim. This is very important because he died for followers of another religion.

▲ *Guru Tegh Bahadur*

1 Explain what the word 'martyr' means. (You can look this up in the Glossary on page 63.)

2 This chapter names 9 of the 10 Gurus (beginning with Nanak). Your teacher should go round the class, giving everyone a number up to 9. Remind yourself about your Guru (eg if you are number 7, then your Guru is Har Rai). On a sheet of paper:

- Put his name and number.
- Draw a picture of him or of something that he did.
- Write a brief statement about him.

Your teacher can collect these in and keep them until you have learnt about the 10th Guru.

3 Sikhs are taught to stand up for the rights of others. The ninth Guru died for this. Choose one way in which you could stand up for other people. Share your idea with a partner.

Guru Gobind Rai and the First Vaisakhi

3

Guru Gobind Rai was the tenth and final human Guru. He later changed his last name to Singh. You will read about this later in the chapter.

Guru Gobind Singh was the only son of the ninth Guru. He was a clever man and a very good soldier. The emperor had killed his father, but he was not afraid to stand up to the emperor. He was concerned for people and wanted them to stand up for their rights.

Guru Gobind Singh was a great leader. He made the Sikhs proud of their religion. He made them strong and brave to defend the weak. He trained them to be soldiers. He saw all this as part of the religion.

He wrote religious poems which spoke of God as the ruler, not emperors:

> . . . God alone is the only Giver and Ruler of all.
> All stand like beggars at his court.
>
> *Guru Gobind Singh*

He taught all Sikhs to have faith in God and in themselves. The emperor sent his army to destroy the Sikhs. But they stood firm. A period of peace followed. Like any good soldier, he used it to grow stronger.

◀ *Guru Gobind Singh, the tenth Guru*

Vaisakhi 1699

> It is through the actions of the Khalsa that I have won all my victories and have been able to help others.
>
> *Guru Gobind Singh*

Large numbers of Sikhs had gathered for the Indian festival of Vaisakhi. But this was to be no ordinary celebration.

Guru Gobind Singh appeared with a sword. He asked for volunteers who would give their heads for him! After a long pause, one man stepped forward. The Guru led him into his tent. The Guru came out with his sword dripping with blood. This happened 4 more times.

After the fifth brave man had come forward, the Guru came out with all 5, unharmed. They had shown that they were willing to give their lives for their religion. This is what all true Sikhs should be like. They were called the Five Beloved Ones.

▲ *Guru Gobind Singh calls for volunteers to give their heads for Sikhism*

The 5 men were the first members of the Sikh community. It was called the Khalsa. They were given some sugar-water called amrit as a sign. Then they gave amrit to the Guru himself and to many others to show that they belonged to the Khalsa.

The Guru gave all these Sikhs a new name. The men were called Singh, which means 'lion'. The women were called Kaur, which means 'princess'. This showed that they were all equal.

> Everyone has eyes, ears and body made out of the same earth, air, fire and water.
>
> *Guru Gobind Singh*

▲ *Modern-day Sikhs act as the Five Beloved Ones*

▲ *Guru Gobind Singh and the Guru Granth Sahib*

Guru Gobind Singh had lived as a soldier, and he met a violent death. He was stabbed by an enemy.

Before his death, he said that there would be no more human Gurus. Instead, the Sikh holy book was to be their Guru, their teacher. So the Adi Granth became known as the Guru Granth Sahib. (Sahib is a term of respect, like 'Sir'.)

Key words

Khalsa
amrit
Singh
Kaur
Guru Granth Sahib

1. Make a list of FIVE things that Guru Gobind Singh did for the Sikhs. In pairs, talk about which you think was the most important and why.
2. Look back at question 2 in Chapter 2. Do the same work, but on Guru Gobind Singh.
3. Discuss: the Five Beloved Ones were willing to give up their lives for their religion. Is there anything that you think is worth dying for? (Think about jobs where people put their lives at risk.)

4 The Khalsa

TASK
Talk about the clubs that you belong to.
What rules do you have to follow?
What did you have to do to join?

The Khalsa belongs to the Lord,
victory to the Lord.

The first members of the Khalsa showed that they were willing to die for Sikhism.

▲ *Sikhs today join the Khalsa in the same way as the Five Beloved Ones. They drink some amrit, and it is sprinkled over them.*

The Guru did not want it to be easy to belong to the Khalsa. He wanted people who would stand firm for their faith. It is still hard today to be a member of the Khalsa and not all Sikhs belong to it.

When Sikhs join the Khalsa, they have to accept its rules. They must accept the teachings of Sikhism. They must live good lives and look after other Sikhs. They must be ready to give up everything for their religion.

They show that they belong to the Khalsa by wearing the Five Ks.

The Five Ks

Kesh – uncut hair
Kangha – a comb
Kara – a steel bracelet
Kachha – shorts
Kirpan – a sword

KESH

► ***Kesh is uncut hair****. It is natural – a gift from God. When tied neatly in a turban, it is a sign of Sikhism that is easy to see*

KANGHA

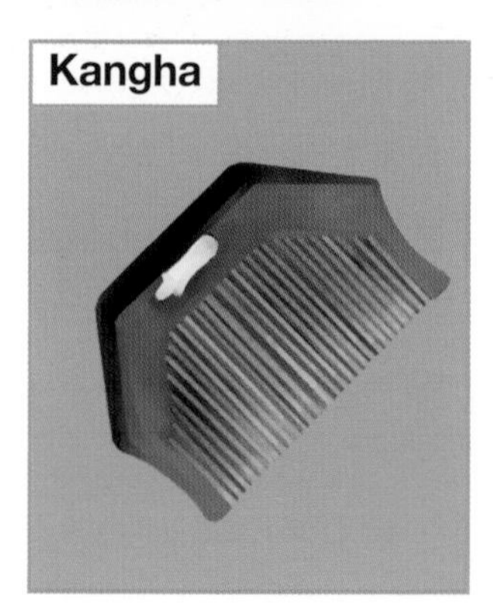

► ***The kangha is a comb****. It is used to keep the hair clean and tidy*

KARA

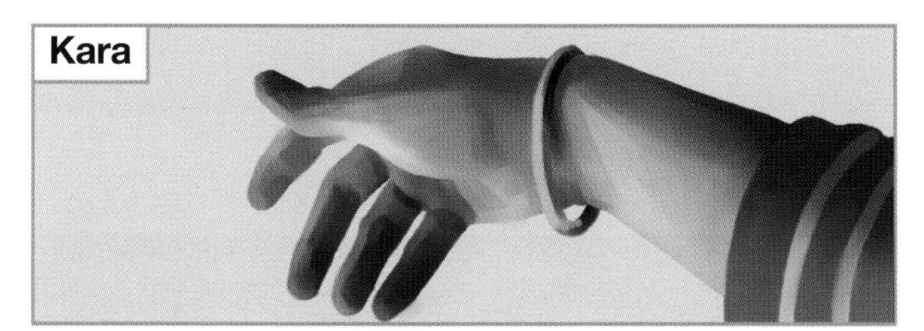

▲ ***The kara is a steel bracelet.*** *It is a symbol. The circle reminds Sikhs of God. Like God, it has no beginning and no end. Steel is strong and Sikhs must be strong in their faith*

KACHHA

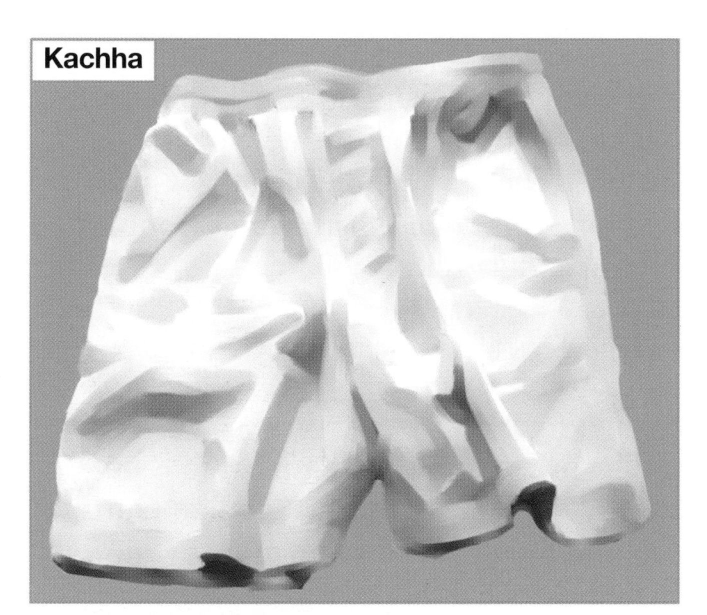

▲ ***Kachha are baggy shorts.*** *They are worn as underwear by both men and women. In the days when the Khalsa first started, they made fighting easier. So they remind Sikhs that they must always be ready to defend their religion and to defend the weak*

> The brave and truly religious have the right to fight and die for a good cause.
>
> *Guru Nanak*

KIRPAN

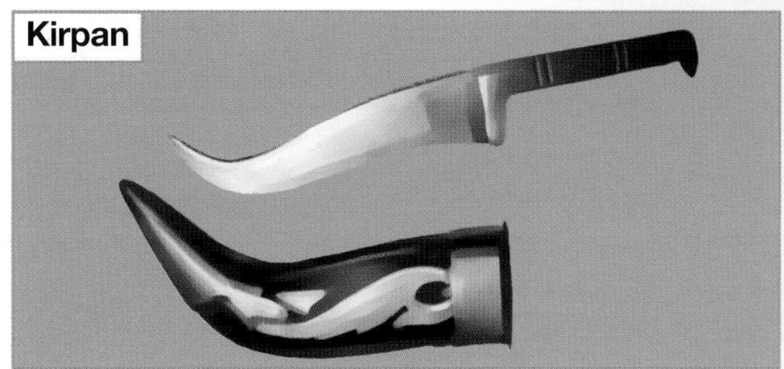

▲ ***The kirpan is a sword.*** *This too reminds the Sikhs that they may sometimes have to fight. Remember that when the Khalsa started, the Sikhs were being attacked by their enemies. Many Sikhs today see it as a symbol of fighting their own inner temptations*

> When all other means to put a stop to tyranny fail, then it is lawful to take up the sword.
>
> *Guru Gobind Singh*
>
> (NB 'tyranny' is a reign of terror.)

1 Draw the Five Ks and write a brief explanation of each.

2 Discuss:

a) Do you think it is ever right to use violence – even in a good cause? Think of some examples to back up your views. They can be real or made up.

b) Can you think of any tyrants in the 20th century who have led a reign of terror? Would it have been right to try to kill them?

3 Khalsa men are given the name Singh. This means 'Lion'. They are to be strong and fearless like a lion, but also gentle and caring. If you could be named after an animal, which would you choose and why?

5 Guru Granth Sahib

► *The Guru Granth Sahib. It is written in the language of the Punjab. This is called Gurmukhi. It has 1430 pages and 3384 hymns*

TASK

Talk about books which are important to you. Why are they important? How do you look after them?

Make a class display:

- Each pupil is to draw the front cover of their chosen book and put the title on it. Also on this cover: write a sentence about the book, and another saying why it is important to you. DO NOT put your name on it. When the display is up, you can guess which books belong to which people in the class.

> He who wants to see the Guru, let him search the Holy Granth.
>
> *Guru Gobind Singh*

After the death of Guru Gobind Singh, there were no more human Gurus. Instead, Sikhs are guided by their holy book. It is called the Guru Granth Sahib. Sikhs believe it is the word of God.

It was Guru Arjan Dev (the fifth Guru) who first put together the holy book. It included the writings of the first 4 Gurus and his own. It also had hymns from Hindu and Muslim poets.

> Without the true Guru, the path is not found.
>
> *Beni*

The present Guru Granth Sahib is not exactly the same as this first book. Guru Gobind Singh added some more hymns, including one of his own.

Today, copies of the Guru Granth Sahib are all the same. The same hymns are on the same page in every copy.

> Nanak, think always in your heart and mind on God's name, that at the last it may rescue you . . .
>
> *Guru Ram Das*

Key words

Gurmukhi **gurdwara**
Dasam Granth

▲ *The Guru Granth Sahib is read from a raised platform*

Sikhs believe the Guru Granth Sahib is the word of God. It is usually kept in their place of worship, called a gurdwara. They treat it with great respect, just like a human Guru:

- It is raised up on a platform (like a throne), under a canopy.
- A person waves a fly-whisk over it, as they would do for someone important in India.
- Sikhs bow down to it before taking their seat. (This is not worshipping it.)
- People sit below it on the floor. It would be rude to point their feet towards it.
- When it is moved, everyone stands.
- It is carried above everyone else, on someone's head.
- Sikhs do not turn their backs on it.
- Sikhs must have a separate room for the Guru Granth Sahib if they keep it at home.

> We treat our Holy Book just like a living Guru. We respect it like a living Guru. It's given a special place in the gurdwara . . . above everyone else!
>
> It guides our lives. When I want advice I get someone to open it for me and the first paragraph on the page will give me the answer.

▲ *Ways of showing respect to the Guru Granth Sahib*

Most Sikhs keep extracts from the Guru Granth Sahib at home. They may have the whole book brought to their house for special occasions.

There is another holy book called the Dasam Granth. This has the writings of Guru Gobind Singh. It is not so important as the Guru Granth Sahib.

> Give me strength, O Lord, to do good deeds.
>
> *Guru Gobind Singh*

Some of Guru Gobind Singh's writings show the hard times in which he lived:

> And when the time comes, I shall die, fighting bravely in battle.
>
> *Guru Gobind Singh*

1 a) Draw a series of pictures to show how the Guru Granth Sahib is treated with great respect. (Look at page 17 as well as the pictures on this page.)

b) Explain why Sikhs treat the Guru Granth Sahib in this way.

2 Talk about the advantages and disadvantages of having a book as your leader and teacher, rather than a person. List your ideas in 2 columns.

3 Invite a Sikh to talk to your class about the Guru Granth Sahib. Prepare some questions beforehand. Ask him or her to tell you some of the teachings of this holy book. Ask what difference it makes to their lives. Ask how they read their holy book at home.

Rahit Maryada 6

When Guru Gobind Singh started the Khalsa, he gave Sikhs rules to live by. Changes were made to this first list. Finally, a list of rules was published in 1945 which is followed by Sikhs today. It is known as the Rahit. This word means 'conduct or discipline'. It has been published in English for Sikhs living in Britain, the USA and Canada.

TASK

Think about the rules you live by.

- Do you have a general rule like 'treat other people as you would like them to treat you'? If so, write it down.
- Make a list of specific rules you try to follow, like 'do not steal', 'do not fight','do not swear' .

Think about where these rules came from. Who gave you your rules for living?

▲ *The meeting place where the Sikh rules were agreed*

▲ *This is a copy of the Rahit. It has the seal of the committee on it*

The Rahit teaches Sikhs what to do and what not to do.

The Rahit is divided into many sections. It covers all parts of a Sikh's life. It starts by saying that a Sikh is anyone who believes in:

- one God
- the 10 gurus and their teachings
- the Guru Granth Sahib
- the amrit ceremony

and is not a member of another religion.

Sikhs must join in with other Sikhs for worship. They must also study the Guru Granth Sahib together.

> Sikhs must visit the places where Sikhs meet for worship and prayer (the gurdwaras), and joining with the others, share in the benefits that study of the holy book gives.
>
> *Rahit*

▲ *These Sikhs are following the Rahit by coming to their place of worship*

The Rahit also covers family life. Here are the kind of rules it has:

Family Life

Sikhs should:

- pray to God before beginning anything;
- bring up their children as Sikhs;
- keep their children's hair long;
- not take drugs of any kind, including alcohol and tobacco;
- not pierce their ears or wear earrings.

A Sikh woman must not cover her face with a veil.

Wider world

Sikhs should:

- earn their living by honest work;
- give to the poor;
- not steal or gamble;
- do voluntary work as part of their religion;
- keep these rules right through their lives.

▲ *Sikh children learn about their religion by singing the hymns from the Guru Granth Sahib*

1 In pairs, read the Sikh rules on this page. Talk about which of these rules you agree with, and why. Which do you disagree with, and why?

2 It is important for Sikhs to do voluntary service. For example, they work in the free kitchens (see page 35) at their places of worship. Write down TWO kinds of voluntary work. Why do people give up their own time to do these things?

7 What Sikhs Believe

God

Sikhs believe in one God. They believe that God made the world. They believe that he loves everyone he has made:

> God is the beginning and end of everything. He is the Designer and Creator.
>
> *Guru Gobind Singh*

> God takes care of all, at all times, birds, beasts, mountains, snakes and kings. God loves all beings in the sea and on the land . . .
>
> *Guru Gobind Singh*

Their main beliefs about God are in a poem written by Guru Nanak, called the 'Mul Mantar'. It is at the beginning of the Guru Granth Sahib. It is said every day in the morning prayer.

ੴ ਸਤਿਨਾਮੁ ਕਰਤਾ ਪੁਰਖੁ ਨਿਰਭਉ ਨਿਰਵੈਰੁ
ਅਕਾਲ ਮੂਰਤਿ ਅਜੂਨੀ ਸੈਭੰ ਗੁਰ ਪ੍ਰਸਾਦਿ ॥

▲ *The 'Mul Mantar' in Gurmukhi*

This is the 'Mul Mantar' in English:

There is One God
Whose Name is Truth.
God is the Creator,
and is without fear and without hate.
God is timeless,
God's Spirit is throughout the universe.
God is not born,
Nor will die to be born again,
God is self-existent.
By the grace of the Gurus God is made
known to mankind.

God's name is very important to Sikhs. They try to remember it at all times. They repeat God's name in the 'Mul Mantar', and think about what it means. You will also often hear them say 'Waheguru' which means 'Wonderful Lord'. This is a way of showing their love for God.

> If you desire eternal happiness of all types devote yourself to God's Name.
>
> *Guru Gobind Singh*

► *This says 'Ik Onkar'. It means 'there is one God.' It is the first line of the 'Mul Mantar'*

Guru

Sikhs believe that they should turn to the Guru Granth Sahib for guidance. Some people say that the word 'guru' is made up of two words. 'Gu' means darkness; and 'ru' means light. So a guru is someone who leads you from darkness to light.

> Without a Guru no one has reached God, for all his talking; it is he who shows the way and teaches true devotion.
>
> *Guru Nanak*

Sikhs look for God's guidance by opening the Guru Granth Sahib anywhere (allowing God to lead them). This is called a 'hukam', meaning 'God's will'. They read from the new section on that page.

Key words

'Mul Mantar'
Ik Onkar
Waheguru
hukam

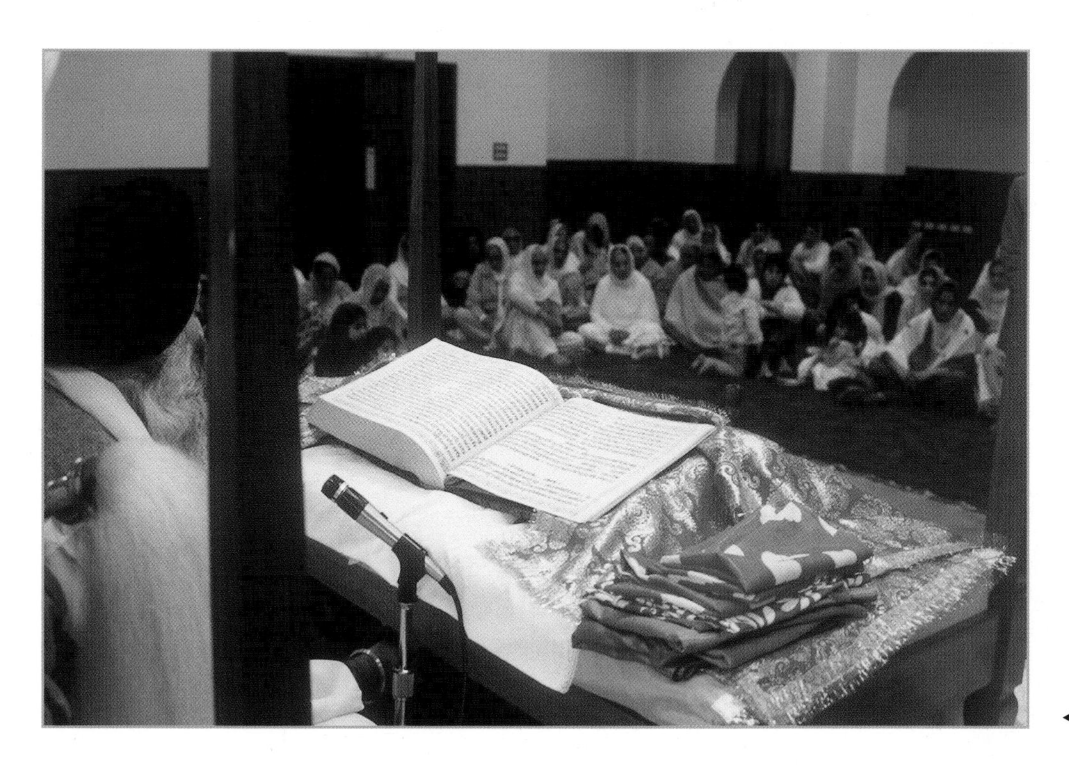

◀ *A hukam being read*

1 Copy the Ik Onkar symbol for Sikhism. Explain what it means.

2 a) Where would you find the 'Mul Mantar'?

b) Explain TWO things that it teaches about God.

3 Write your own poem about your beliefs.

Reincarnation and the goal of life

> One who seeks pleasure wanders from birth to birth, not caring about God's Will.
>
> *Guru Nanak*

Sikhs believe in reincarnation. This means being reborn again and again. Sikhism teaches that people's selfish ways tie them to this earth.

Sikhs do not want to be reborn again and again and again. **Sikhs want to break free from reincarnation. They want to be united with God when they die.**

Sikhs believe that God will set them free from rebirth if they think about him as much as possible and worship him.

> There are links between your present life and your past life. The soul does not die. It takes forward traces of how it behaved in its past lives. But neither you nor your soul remembers this. This life gives you the chance to put right things you did wrong in past lives. Then God might free you from rebirth ... Only God knows when you will be united again with him.
>
> *Guru Gobind Singh*

▼ *Sikhs believe that these things will make them be reborn*

1 Discuss:

a) What do Sikhs believe about reincarnation?

b) Do you think there is any evidence for reincarnation?

c) What do you think happens when we die?

2 In pairs, list TEN things that Sikhs believe are wrong and could cause them to be reborn. (Look again at the rules from the Rahit on page 21.)

Being a Sikh – Birth and Initiation 8

Birth

When a baby is born, the family go to the gurdwara (the place of worship) to name the baby. The ceremony usually happens at the end of the service. The parents bring the baby out and stand in front of the Guru Granth Sahib. Special hymns of thanks are sung.

> God has sent this wonderful gift. Conceived by love may he live many years.
>
> *Guru Arjan Dev*

▲ *The Guru Granth Sahib has been opened at random*

The Guru Granth Sahib is opened at random. The hymn on that page is read out. (Do you remember that this is called a hukam?) The child's name must begin with the first letter of the hymn. The parents choose the name. It can be the same name for a boy or girl.

Prayers of joy are read out before the final prayer of the service. Then everyone shares in a mixture of sugar, water, butter and semolina or flour. It is called Karah Prashad. The baby's family pays for this food on this occasion.

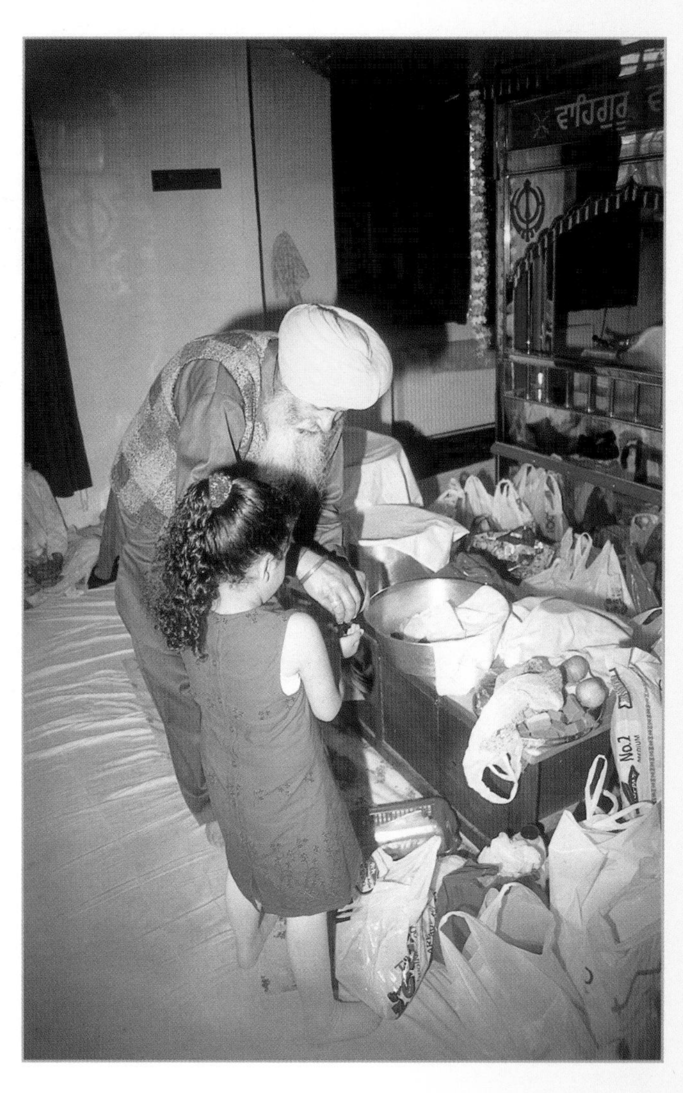

▶ *A young Sikh child is given Karah Parshad*

Sometimes sugar-water (amrit) is made. The beginning of the Guru Granth Sahib is read out. A kirpan (sword) may be dipped in the amrit and put on the baby's tongue. Amrit is used when an adult becomes a Sikh. So it reminds the parents that they should bring up their child as a Sikh. It also shows the sweetness of the word of God.

The parents usually buy presents for the gurdwara. They are often beautiful covers for the Guru Granth Sahib, called romala. A family may also arrange for the Guru Granth Sahib to be brought to their home and read right through.

◀ *Amrit is put on the baby's tongue with the tip of a kirpan*

1 Make a list of what is done in Sikhism for a new baby.

2 In pairs:

a) Why do you think many people want to have a special ceremony for a newborn baby?

b) Make up a ceremony of your own for the birth of a child. Design an invitation card to it, telling people the purpose of the ceremony.

3 a) What reasons do people have for choosing particular names? (Find out why your name was chosen.)

b) If you could choose your name now, what would you choose and why?

Key words

Karah Parshad
romala

The Amrit ceremony

This is the most important ceremony for Sikhs. It shows they are ready to accept all the rules of Sikhism. They become members of the Khalsa.

This ceremony was started by Guru Gobind Singh at Vaisakhi in 1699 CE (see page 12). Today, 5 Sikh men dress up for this ceremony. These remind people of the first Five Beloved Ones.

The ceremony usually takes place in private, in the gurdwara. The Guru Granth Sahib is read. The Sikhs who are joining the Khalsa are asked if they:

- are willing to read, learn and live by the Sikh teachings;
- will pray only to the one God;
- will serve the whole of humanity.

When they have agreed, a prayer is said. Then a hukam is read from the holy book. The amrit is now prepared. The sugar and water are mixed together in an iron bowl by the Five Beloved Ones. They kneel around the bowl and stir the amrit with a double-edged sword, called a khanda. They say prayers from the Guru Granth Sahib.

▲ *The main badge of Sikhism (the Khanda)*

The candidates come forward one by one and kneel by the bowl of amrit. The amrit is sprinkled over them. They drink a handful of amrit 5 times. Each time they say:

- Waheguru ji ka Khalsa,
  Waheguru ji ki Fateh.

This means:

The Khalsa belongs to the Lord,
victory to the Lord.

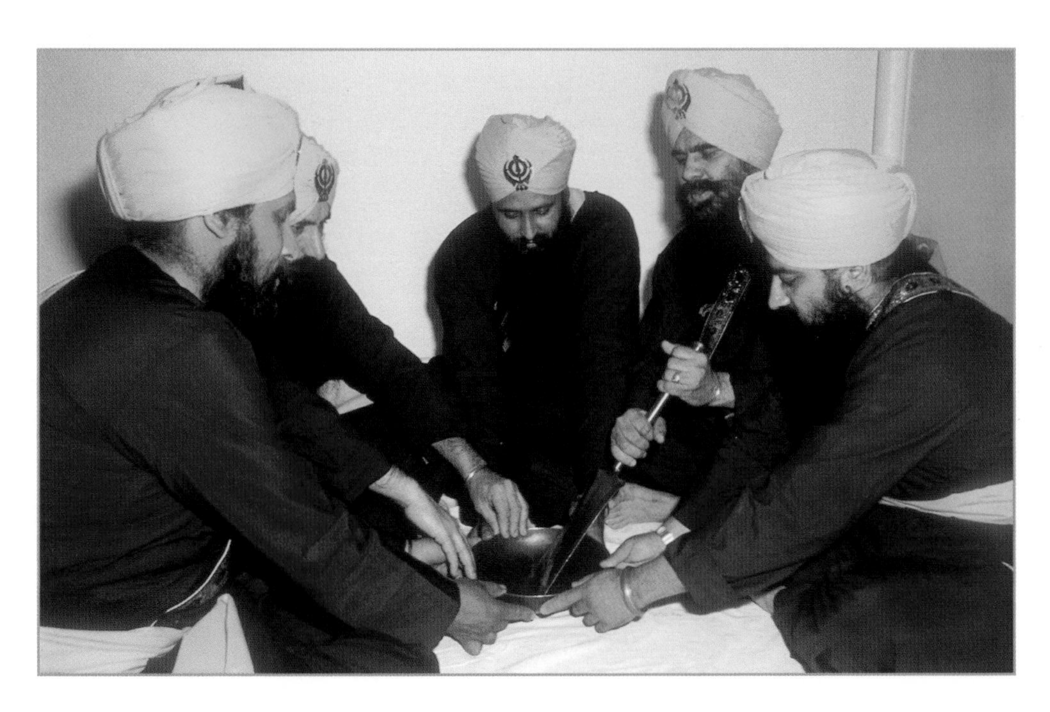

◀ *The Five Beloved Ones at an Amrit ceremony*

◀ *The Amrit ceremony*

The 'Mul Mantar' is said 5 times, and the rules of the Khalsa are explained to the new members. The ceremony ends with the final prayer and another reading from the Guru Granth Sahib. Then they share Karah Parshad together.

- **Khalsa Sikhs must** support other Sikhs and treat everyone equally. They must be peaceful and good-tempered. They must earn money honestly and share with the poor.
- **Khalsa Sikhs must not** smoke, take drugs or drink alcohol. They must not commit adultery. They must not gamble or tell lies.
- Khalsa Sikhs wear the Five Ks.
- Not all Sikhs join the Khalsa. But some may still have uncut hair and keep some of the rules of the Khalsa.
- Others may worship regularly at the gurdwara but not wear the Five Ks or keep the other rules.
- Yet others were born as Sikhs but do not practise their religion.

1 Look at the pictures of the Amrit ceremony. Write a caption for each picture, to describe what is happening.

2 Look at the rules of the Khalsa on this page.
a) Which would you find easy to obey?
b) Which would you find difficult?

3 Have you been through any joining ceremonies? If so:
a) Were they taken by someone special? (Like the Five Beloved Ones.)
b) Did you have to do something unusual? (Like drinking the amrit.)
c) Did you have to make any promises? (Like the rules of the Khalsa.)

► *A Sikh girl reading her daily prayers. These are called 'nit nem', which means 'daily rule'*

Prayers must be said at home in the morning, evening and last thing at night. These are set prayers. Sikhs learn Gurmukhi so that they can say the prayers and read the holy books. A Sikh explains:

> We pray to try to become more like the Gurus. ... We say prayers in the morning, evening and last thing at night. We shouldn't ask for things for ourselves. We end by asking for our sins to be forgiven, and for everything to be good for everyone.

Any time is a good time to read a hukam, but Sikhs will try to read one first thing in the morning. As well as picking these readings at random, Sikhs try to read through the Guru Granth Sahib on a regular basis.

Some Sikh homes do not have a separate room where they can keep the Guru Granth Sahib. They will keep a small book of extracts from it at home. This is used for daily readings. It is treated with respect, and kept in a special place in the home.

Sikhs learn about their religion in the home and in the gurdwara. They can find out about other religions too. They welcome anyone to join them in the gurdwara and to share a meal afterwards.

▼ *A small collection of hymns from the Guru Granth Sahib, called the Gutka. Sikhs keep this at home if they do not have room for the full holy book*

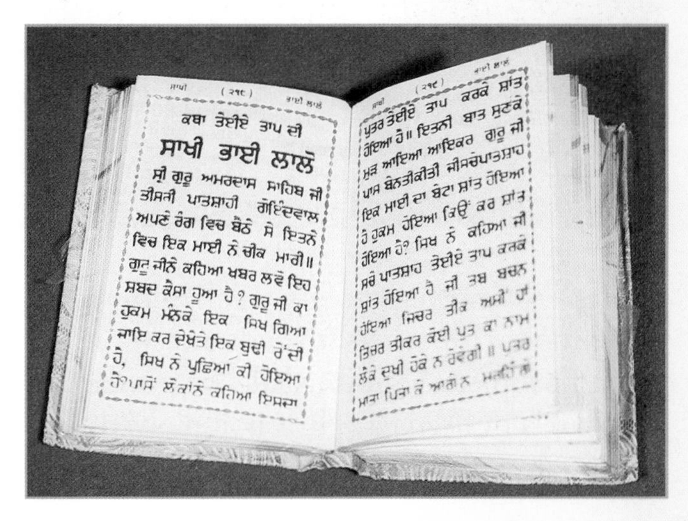

Serving others is very important in Sikhism. Service is not just to other Sikhs. They should treat everyone as their brothers and sisters. There are 3 types of service:

1 **Working with your mind**
This can include teaching about Sikhism. Sikhs can also do this service by belonging to the gurdwara committee, which decides how it is run.

2 **Physical work**
This can include cooking and serving food in the 'free kitchen' or langar. (There is more about the langar on page 35.) It takes a lot of work to feed everyone after the service.

3 **Giving away money and other things**
Most Sikhs give to charities of all sorts.

- When you become a member of the Khalsa you have to show everyone you love them. You do this by doing things to help them, by caring.
- It's important for all people to share in doing all sorts of jobs. We don't believe in the class system, so it's right for somebody who is rich or clever to do ordinary things, like cooking and serving food in the kitchen.
- No work should be below anyone's dignity ... if you need a volunteer for any job every Sikh should step forward ... it's an honour to serve others.

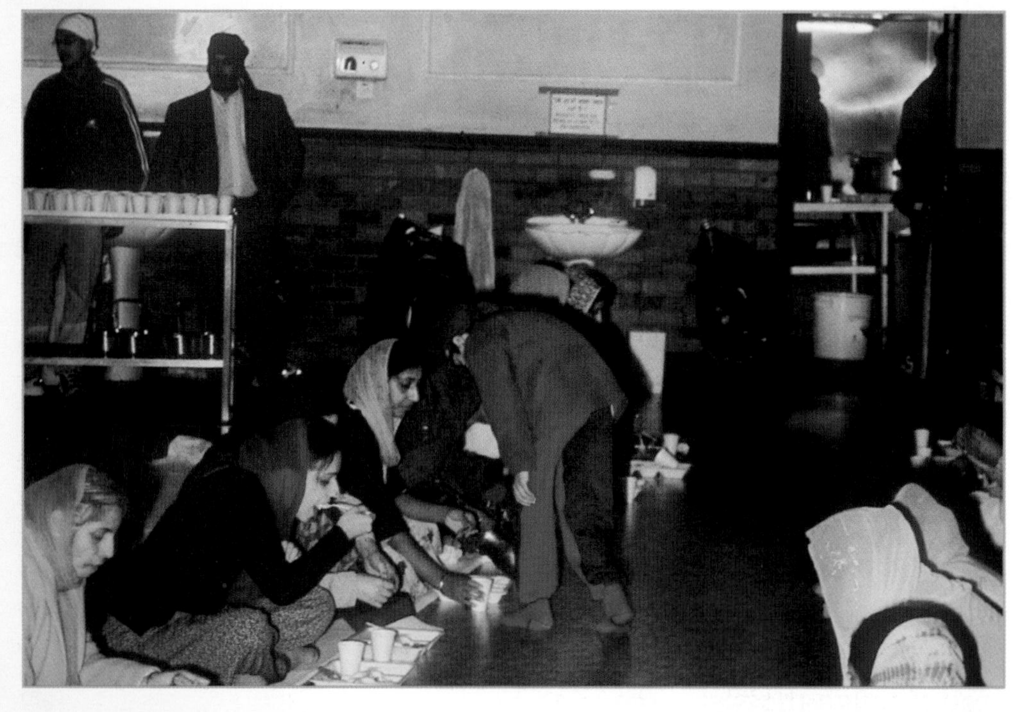

◀ *A young Sikh serves food*

▼ *Food is prepared which will not offend anyone*

Most Sikhs are vegetarians. When they share food with others, they do not want to offend people. So it is usually vegetarian. Alcohol is not served. It is not allowed because it makes people lose control.

Sikhs should dress modestly. The Punjabi suit is popular with women. It has long baggy trousers (shalwar) and a long tunic (kameez). All Khalsa Sikhs, men and women, must wear the Five Ks. These can be worn with most styles of dress.

> Sikhism is a practical religion; wearing the Five Ks is essential. Everyone can see me and know what I believe and stand for. It shows what I really think is important. If somebody said I couldn't wear them, I don't know what I'd do.

Many Sikh men wear a turban. It is not one of the Five Ks, but it is important. All the Sikh Gurus wore turbans and the Guru Granth Sahib says that it completes the appearance of a Sikh. Under the Race Relations Act, Sikhs who wear turbans do not have to wear a crash-helmet when riding a motorcycle.

◀ *Young Sikhs with their teachers, all in traditional dress*

1 a) Explain why voluntary service is important to Sikhs.

b) Design a poster that could be put up in a gurdwara. It should encourage Sikhs to do voluntary service.

2 Discuss:

a) Read the quotation on this page. Why is it important for Khalsa Sikhs to wear the Five Ks?

b) Can you think of any difficulties there may be in wearing them in this country? (You will need to remind yourself of the Five Ks in Chapter 4.)

10 Worship and The Gurdwara

> Sikhs should visit the gurdwara as often as possible
>
> *Rahit*

A Sikh place of worship is called a gurdwara. This means 'the door to the Guru'. It is the place where the Guru Granth Sahib is kept. It is where Sikhs can hear the teachings of the Gurus.

Gurdwaras differ in size and shape, but they all have a tall flag-pole outside. This has an orange flag with the symbol of Sikhism on it. The flag is called the Nishan Sahib. The symbol on the flag is called the Khanda. It takes its name from the double-edged sword in the middle (which is also called a khanda). But it also has a circle and 2 outer swords. (You can see a picture of it on page 27.)

Before you get too far inside a gurdwara, you have to take off your shoes. This is a sign of respect. It also shows that you are leaving the everyday world behind you. And it helps to keep the place clean. Both men and women must also cover their heads. There may be a notice telling you not to bring in tobacco or alcohol.

Inside, the worship hall is often large with lots of space. There may be some pictures of the Gurus, but these are not worshipped. The main focus is the raised platform and canopy at the front. This may be decorated with tinsel and streamers. It is where the *Guru Granth Sahib* is read from. When it is not being read, it is covered with beautiful cloths called romalas. People often give these to the gurdwara on special occasions like the birth of a child.

▲ *The Nishan Sahib shows that this is a gurdwara*

▲ *Inside the worship hall of a gurdwara*

The person who reads the *Guru Granth Sahib* is called a granthi. He or she sits on the platform behind the holy book. Someone often stands waving a fan made from hair. This shows how important the holy book is.

▲ *The granthi is reading from the Guru Granth Sahib. The fan can be seen behind him*

The Guru Granth Sahib is treated with great respect. There is always a room where it is laid to rest at night. This is usually a private room high in the gurdwara. It has a bed covered with romalas. At the end of the day, the holy book is carefully wrapped in a clean cloth. The head of the granthi is covered with another clean cloth, and the holy book is carried on his head. Everyone stands as the book is taken out. Next morning it is brought back to the worship hall.

▲ *The Guru Granth Sahib being taken from the Golden Temple at night to its place of rest*

There may be several other rooms in the gurdwara. Some are used for meetings. There may be classrooms, a library and a museum. The granthi and others who work at the gurdwara may have flats there to live in.

1 Draw the Khanda symbol that is seen on Sikh flags (see page 27).

2 Describe what you can see in the worship hall in the photo.

3 Imagine you are a teacher planning a visit to a gurdwara. You need to prepare your pupils beforehand. Using the information in this chapter, tell them:

a) How they should dress for the visit.

b) What they would have to do when they entered the gurdwara.

c) How they should behave in the worship hall.

d) What they should expect to be given.

4 If you went on a visit to a gurdwara, what would you most like to ask the granthi?

Worship

There is no set day for worship. It takes place most days. The main day for worship in Britain is Sunday, because this is when most people do not work.

▲ *The singers play traditional Sikh instruments: drum and harmonium*

▲ *Sikhs bow down and make offerings when they come into the worship hall*

When Sikhs enter the worship hall, they come straight to the front. They bow before the holy book and put some money in a special box. Then they take their seat. The women usually sit on one side, with the children. The men sit on the other side. Everyone sits on the floor, below the holy book. They cross their legs.

Worship is mainly the singing of hymns from the Guru Granth Sahib. The singers do this and make music. The people listen and think about the meaning of the words. Sometimes the singers explain the hymns before singing them. There may also be talks about Sikhism.

Karah Parshad is prepared before the service. It is brought into the worship hall and placed near the Guru Granth Sahib. It is shared out at the end of the service.

These words from the Guru Granth Sahib are read near the end of the service:

> Our right and wrong deeds will be judged at Your court.
> Some will be seated near Your seat; some will be kept distant for ever.
> The work has ended for those who have worshipped You.
> O Nanak, their faces are lit with joy,
> and they set free many others.

Key words

Nishan Sahib
Khanda
granthi

The Langar

> Let all share equally; no one should be seen as an outsider.
>
> *Guru Arjan Dev*

TASK

Equality means that people have the same rights and are treated with the same respect. Do you think that everyone is equal in our society? Can you think of reasons and examples where people are treated differently?

The Sikh langar shows the importance of equality in Sikhism. A langar is a free kitchen. Guru Nanak started them for these reasons:

- to make sure that Sikhs from all different backgrounds would mix and eat together;
- to give food to those who had come a long way to hear him;
- to feed the poor.

Before long it became the custom to give visitors a meal before meeting for prayer. They all sat down together, however important they were. Others were needed to cook and serve the food. This was their service to others. Everybody took a turn, no matter which background they came from.

Today langars are much the same. While worship is going on, some Sikhs are working in the kitchen. Both men and women do this. The service is often relayed to them using loudspeakers. They prepare food for everyone at the gurdwara. Prayers are said at the end of the service to bless this food.

If you visit a gurdwara, you will be offered food and drink. It is rude to refuse it.

▲ *Everyone sits to eat at the same level. This shows that they are all equal*

1 a) In pairs, make a list of all the things that go on in a gurdwara. Decide how many rooms are needed.

b) Design a new gurdwara. Draw a plan of it. Label all the rooms, saying what they are for.

2 Discuss if your school could learn anything from Sikhism about equality. (For example, do you have a school council so that all pupils can have a say in how the school is run?)

11 Sikhs Celebrating

Sikhs have special ways of celebrating. The Guru Granth Sahib is central in many of these.

One way of celebrating an important occasion is to have a reading of the Guru Granth Sahib right through without stopping. This is called an Akhand Path. It takes about 48 hours and is done by a team of readers. It begins 2 days before the important event. It ends on the morning of the important day.

The Guru Granth Sahib may also be taken in procession through the streets. A place for the holy book may be set up on a lorry, just like in the gurdwara. It is raised up on cushions under a canopy. (In a way, the lorry becomes a gurdwara – a gurdwara is where the Guru Granth Sahib is kept.) It is driven slowly through the streets with 5 Khalsa Sikhs in full dress walking in front. These are called the Five Beloved Ones (see page 12). Often hundreds of people follow behind.

▲ *An Akhand Path*

Sat siri Akal!
Victory to the True Lord!

Key words

Akhand Path
bhangra

► *What can you see in this photo?*

At other times, the Nishan Sahib plays an important part. This is the Sikh flag. The flag is taken down and the flag-pole is washed in water and yoghurt. A new flag is put back. The old flag is torn up. Sikhs treasure any piece they are able to get. While this goes on, hymns are sung and prayers are said.

▲ *The flag-pole is being washed*

Sport is often part of a celebration. The Gurus wanted Sikhs to play sports. They needed to be fit in case they had to fight. Today, they play team games like hockey and football. There may also be wrestling matches and running races at festivals.

▲ *Bhangra dancers*

There may be competitions for martial arts or table tennis. Sometimes there are trials of strength. Bhangra dancing is very popular with Sikhs. Dancers dress in loose, brightly coloured costumes. It is very energetic. They dance to a drum beat. They may twirl sharp swords as they dance.

1 Copy and complete:
At the centre of many Sikh celebrations is the Guru _______ Sahib. An important way to celebrate is to have an Akhand _______. This is the non-stop ___________ of the holy book. It takes about ________ hours to complete.

2 a) Look at the photo of the procession with the Guru Granth Sahib. Describe everything you can see in the picture.

b) Have you ever taken part in a public procession? If so, how did you feel?

3 In pairs, discuss the good things about taking part in sports.

12 Festivals

Most Sikh festivals are anniversaries of the lives of the 10 Gurus. They are called gurpurbs, which means 'Guru-days'. If you look at the list below, you will see the most important ones. Two days celebrate births and 2 celebrate deaths. Others are to do with important events in their lives.

There is usually a non-stop reading of the Guru Granth Sahib (an Akhand Path) before the days of the births and deaths of Gurus. Then they are celebrated in the usual worship in the gurdwara. Hymns written by that Guru will be sung. There may also be a talk about his life.

FESTIVAL	ENGLISH CALENDAR DATE
Birth of Guru Nanak	November
Birth of Guru Gobind Singh	5 January
Hola Mahalla	14 March
Vaisakhi	14 April
Martyrdom of Guru Arjan	16 June
Martyrdom of Guru Tegh Bahadur	24 November
Diwali	October/November

▲ *The main Sikh festivals*

Vaisakhi

▲ *A recent poster advertising Vaisakhi. 1999 was the 300th anniversary of the Khalsa in 1699*

Vaisakhi is the most important Sikh festival. It marks the start of the Khalsa. It is also the Sikh new year. It is also a Hindu new year and harvest festival.

Vaisakhi falls on 14 April. In Britain it is usually celebrated on the following Sunday.

The Sikh flag is replaced. There is a procession with the Guru Granth Sahib. There may be a fair with sports and bhangra dancing. There may be an exhibition of Sikh life. Amrit ceremonies are often held at this time. Can you think why? (Look back at page 27.)

Diwali

This festival is also celebrated by Hindus. It is a festival of lights. But it has a different meaning for Sikhs. They remember an important event in the life of Guru Hargobind (the sixth Guru). The story goes that he was about to be set free from prison. But he didn't want to leave behind 52 Hindu princes who were in prison with him. He asked if he could take with him as many as could cling to his robes. He left the prison with all 52 clinging to the tassles of his coat! So Diwali is a celebration of freedom and human rights. It reminds us that Sikhs try to help others, even if they are from another religion.

▲ *Guru Hargobind leaving the prison*

▲ *Sikhs light candles at Diwali to remember the release of Guru Hargobind*

Hola Mohalla

This Sikh spring festival is called Hola Mohalla. Guru Gobind Singh started it as a time for military training. Today it is celebrated mainly in the Punjab, with sports. Few people celebrate it in Britain.

1 Match the name of the festival with its meaning:

gurpurbs	start of the Khalsa
Vaisakhi	freedom
Diwali	Guru-days

2 Diwali and Vaisakhi were both important Hindu festivals. How have Sikhs made them into Sikh celebrations?

3 Look at the poster on Vaisakhi for ideas. Then design a poster to advertise one of the other Sikh festivals. It should tell people what the festival is for and how it will be celebrated.

4 Think about festivals that you celebrate. How are they similar to Sikh festivals, and how do they differ? Make notes in TWO columns.

13 Being a Sikh – Marriage and Funerals

Marriage

All the Gurus were married, except one who died young. Guru Nanak compared the worshipper's love of God, to the love of a husband and wife:

> Listen Lord-Husband/Wife, this soul is lonely in the wilderness!
>
> My Beloved . . . how may I find peace without You?
>
> *Guru Nanak,* Guru Granth Sahib

Sikh marriages are usually arranged. This means that the parents find a partner for their son or daughter – although they must agree with the choice. They look for someone with a similar background, education and interests. This Sikh woman felt they made the right choice:

> It wasn't so much arranged as agreed. Other members of the family knew me in ways I didn't know myself. I might have made a bad choice – for the wrong reasons. No, I don't have any regrets – they were right!

> I love my parents and I knew they wouldn't do anything to hurt me. So when they said I should get married, I didn't want to let them down, even though I wanted my own career. ... I never imagined I'd be this happy. Now my husband is more important to me than my career.

▲ *The bride and groom wear red and gold – the colours of happiness*

▲ *The families bring each other gifts*

The wedding takes place in the bride's home or the local gurdwara. It must be done in the presence of the Guru Granth Sahib. Before the wedding ceremony begins, members of both families meet. They sing hymns and give each other gifts.

The bride and groom are given advice about married life.

The couple and their parents stand as a prayer is said to bless them. They all bow towards the Guru Granth Sahib to show that they agree to the marriage. The bride's father puts garlands of flowers over the couple. He puts one end of the groom's scarf into the bride's hand.

> They are not husband and wife who only live together.
> True husband and wife are those who have one spirit in 2 bodies.
> *Guru Amar Das*

▲ *Walking round the* Guru Granth Sahib

The marriage hymn is read out. It has 4 verses. At the end of each verse, the couple walk round the Guru Granth Sahib. Then they bow to the holy book to show that they accept its teachings. After the final walk round the Guru Granth Sahib, people may throw flower petals over the couple.

The newly-weds are welcomed by their parents with sweets and garlands. People come forward to congratulate them. Gifts of money are put in their laps. It is to help them at the start of their married life. Everyone then leaves to share a meal.

1 Draw a picture-strip of SIX things that happen at a Sikh wedding. Explain what is happening beneath each picture.

2 In the second quote, the woman said that her family knew her better than she knew herself. How well do your friends know you? Working with a friend, each write down what the other person is like. Then discuss what each has written.

3 In an arranged marriage, the 2 families become very close. Discuss:

a) What parts of the marriage ceremony show this?

b) What are the advantages of having both families behind the marriage? Can you think of any disadvantages?

Funerals

> Each day that dawns must reach its end;
> All must leave, for none may stay.
> Our friends take their leave, we must also go.
> Death is our fate, our journey long.
>
> *Ravidas*, Guru Granth Sahib
>
> Man is proud of physical strength, wealth . . .
> None of these shall be his in death.
>
> *Guru Nanak*

Sikhs are taught to accept death as the natural end of this life. They believe that death is not the end of everything. They hope their loved ones are united with God when they die. If not, they will be reborn.

Even people who have a firm faith will be sad when someone close to them dies. Sikhs turn to the Guru Granth Sahib for comfort. Hymns from the holy book are sung at the funeral. The whole of the Guru Granth Sahib is read during the period of mourning.

When a Sikh dies, the body is washed and dressed in clean clothes. If the person was a Khalsa Sikh, then the Five Ks are worn. The body is cremated, which means that it is burnt to ashes. In the Punjab, a son or close relative will light the funeral pyre. In Britain, cremation takes place in a crematorium. Before going there, a service is held at the gurdwara. Friends and relatives can come and say goodbye.

The period of mourning lasts up to 10 days. This is the time when those who are most affected by the death can come to terms with it. It ends with the sharing of Karah Parshad. After that, people go back to their normal lives.

> When I am gone, sing only those hymns which lead worshippers to freedom from rebirth.
>
> *Sundar*

This is from the final prayers that are said.

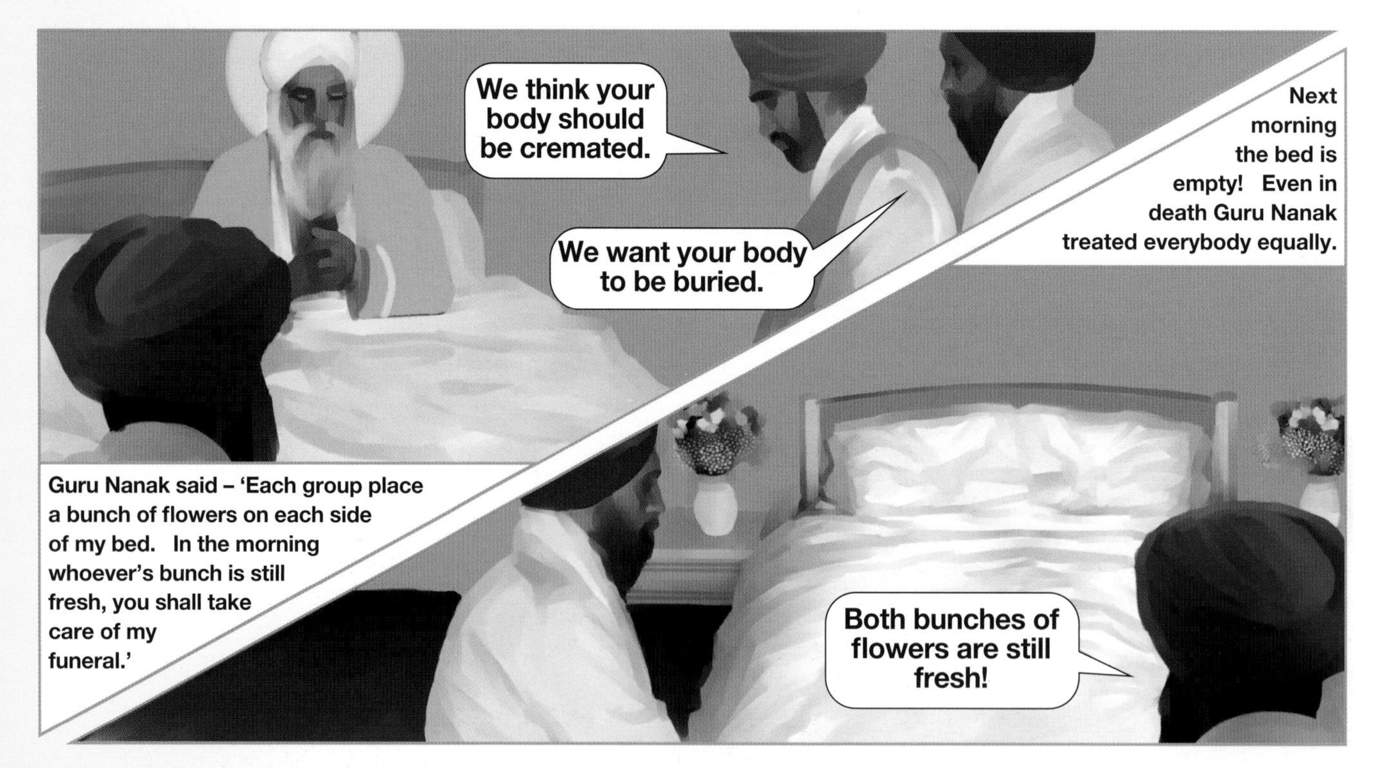

▲ *There is a story about Guru Nanak's death which helps to show his belief that all people are equal. Even in death Guru Nanak did not show any favouritism to Hindu or Muslim followers*

◀ *A Sikh funeral*

Sikhs do not have memorial stones to remember the person who has died. Often the ashes are sprinkled on flowing water, though they may be buried.

The dawn of a new day
Is the messenger of a sunset,
Earth is not our permanent home.
Life is like a shadow on a wall.

1 Discuss:

a) How does this quote on this page explain why Sikhs do not have memorials of the dead?

b) Do you think it is sometimes helpful for those left behind to have memorials? Explain your ideas.

2 a) Where do Sikhs turn for comfort when someone has died? Try to find TWO answers.

b) Who might you turn to for comfort at a time of great sadness? Can you think of any examples?

3 Look carefully at the photo above of a Sikh funeral.

a) Describe what you can see.

b) Why do you think there are bright colours and decorations, rather than sad colours?

Amritsar

▲ *The Golden Temple set in the middle of the Holy Pool*

Amritsar is in the Punjab in India. It is the centre of Sikhism. Amritsar means 'pool of nectar'. It is built on land that Guru Ram Das bought. A natural pool was there already, but Guru Ram Das enlarged it. He wanted it to be a big tank that Sikhs could bathe in. His youngest son, Guru Arjan Dev, continued the building. He built a temple in the middle of the tank. This temple has several Sikh names, but it has become known world-wide as the Golden Temple. This is because it is covered with sheets of gold. Much of the beautiful artwork on the ceilings and doors is also gold.

Sikh places of worship are not really temples. Temples usually have images of God and are places of sacrifice. This is a gurdwara, where the Guru Granth Sahib is kept.

The Golden Temple is built so that worshippers have to step down to enter. This shows the importance of being humble before God. There are also doors on all 4 sides. This shows that Sikhism is open to everyone, not just Sikhs – even the foundation stone was laid by a good Muslim, not a Sikh.

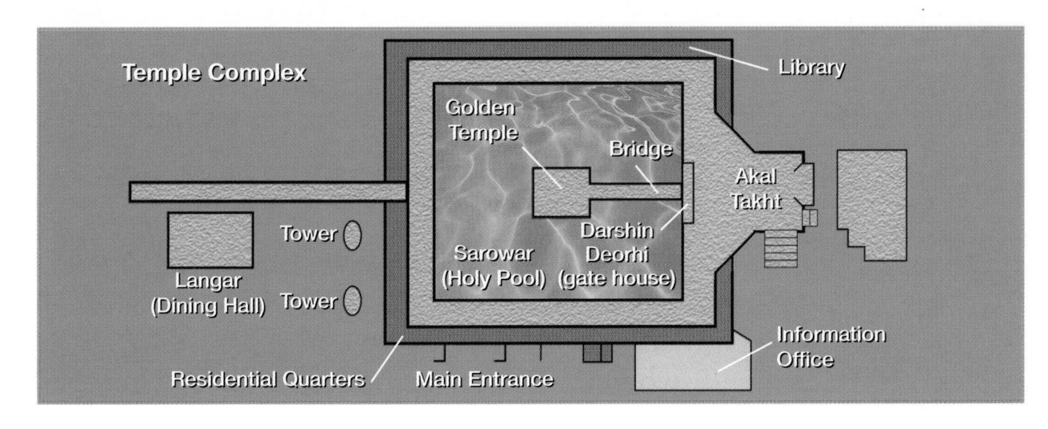

◀ *Plan of the area around the Golden Temple*

You will see from the plan that there are other buildings around the tank. The Guru Granth Sahib is kept in one of these at night. Every morning, it is taken in procession across the bridge to the Golden Temple. It is placed on a platform, under a canopy, with a rail around it. Many visitors walk around it. Meanwhile a copy of the holy book is being read non-stop on the upper floor of the Golden Temple.

As in all gurdwaras, worshippers remove their shoes and cover their heads. They must wash their feet before entering the outer area. They bow as they enter the Golden Temple. They leave gifts inside the rail. And they are given Karah Parshad as they leave.

Many also visit the nearby museum. It has many important things to do with Sikhism.

The Golden Temple is very beautiful. It lifts people's spirits. It deepens their religious feelings.

- When I went to the Golden Temple I felt really happy. It was like being close to God.
- Just being there, I felt . . . at peace . . . contented . . . it made me feel good inside.

▲ *Inside the Golden Temple. A granthi looks after the Guru Granth Sahib as visitors pay their respects*

1 a) How does the Golden Temple show that it is open to everyone?

b) How does it show visitors that they must be humble before God?

2 Make a postcard. Draw or stick onto it a picture of the Golden Temple on one side. Put a message on the other side as if you were there.

3 Have you ever felt 'at peace ... contented' in a special place? If so, talk with a friend about where this was and why it made you feel like this.

4 a) Look at the photo of the Golden Temple. Choose at least FOUR words to describe it.

b) What is the most beautiful place you have ever visited? Can you find a picture of it to stick into your book?

The Five Takhts

The word 'takht' usually means 'throne'. (It is used to describe the raised part for the Guru Granth Sahib, under the canopy.) The Five Takhts are places of Sikh leadership. Many important decisions are taken in local gurdwaras. But decisions that affect all Sikhs are taken by the leaders of the Five Takhts. For example, they can give guidance on the meaning of passages of the Guru Granth Sahib.

The table below tells you what they are called and where they are found.

Name	Place
Akal Takht	Amritsar
Takht Keshgarh	Anandpur
Takht Hazur	Nanded
Takht Harimandir	Patna
Takht Damdama Sahib	Talwandi Sabo

Akal Takht

The name means 'Throne of the timeless one' ie 'throne of God'. This building faces the Golden Temple. Guru Hargobind started to build it.

Inside Akal Takht is a large throne which stands for Sikh rule. This place probably has most influence over Sikh decisions. It is where most of the important Sikh conferences have been held since the last of the human Gurus.

The Other Takhts

The other four Takhts are all connected with Guru Gobind Singh:

1 Anandpur is where he started the Khalsa.
2 Nanded is where he was killed.
3 Patna is where he was born.
4 Talwandi is where he made the final version of the Guru Granth Sahib.

◀ *Akal Takht. There are 2 Sikh flags outside, showing that this is a gurdwara. Worship takes place here every day*

Important Gurdwaras

This chart shows some other important gurdwaras in Sikhism. They are connected with particular Gurus.

Name	Place	Guru
Nankana Sahib	near Lahore	Guru Nanak
Darbar Sahib	Tarn Taran	Guru Arjan Dev
(None given)	Kartarpur	Guru Nanak
Baoli Sahib	Goindwal	Guru Amar Das
Sis Ganj	Delhi	Guru Tegh Bahadur

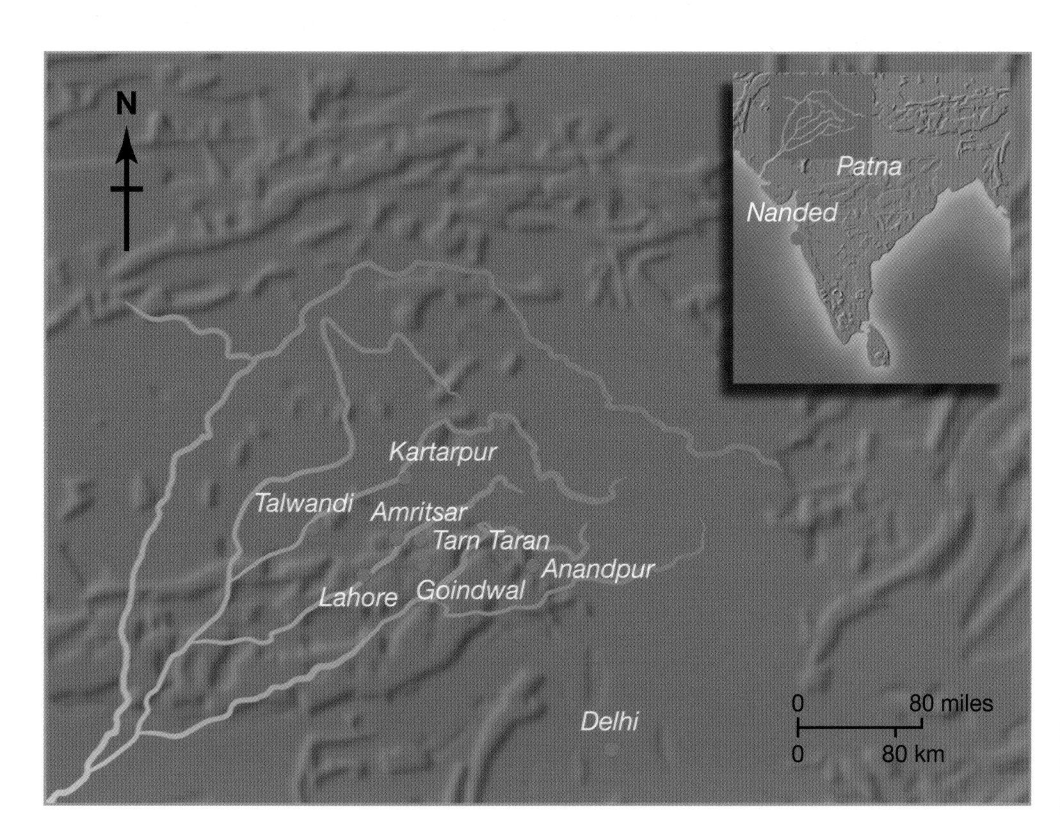

◀ *This map shows where the Five Takhts and the important gurdwaras can be found*

1 a) Find where the Five Takhts are on the map.
b) Find where the important gurdwaras are on the map.

2 The Sikh religion does not ask Sikhs to visit these Sikh places. But many Sikhs do. They particularly want to visit the Golden Temple in Amritsar.
a) Why do you think people like to visit places connected with their history or beliefs?
b) Are there any places that you would like to visit because they have special meaning for you?

▶ *This is the Khanda. It is the symbol on Sikh flags*

- It is named after the double-edged sword in the middle (also called a khanda). This is used in the Amrit ceremony. It reminds Sikhs of their commitment to their religion.
- The circle stands for God, without beginning or end. It also stands for Sikh unity.
- The 2 outer swords stand for the 2 types of authority of the Gurus. They were both religious and political leaders. Today, Sikhism is still a whole way of life.

A martyr is someone who dies for his or her beliefs. They inspire others to be brave. There were many Sikh martyrs in the early days of Sikhism.

Mai Bhago

Mai Bhago was a Sikh woman who lived at the time of Guru Gobind Singh.

The emperor saw the Guru as an enemy. He told the Sikhs to leave Anandpur. He said that those who gave up Sikhism would not be hurt. Forty Sikhs deserted the Guru.

Mai Bhago was very upset when she heard this. She met the 40 men and changed their minds. She led them back to the Guru. On the way, they met the emperor's army. They fought so bravely that the army had to give way. All 40 Sikhs lost their lives in the battle. Mai Bhago was badly wounded but survived.

Guru Gobind Singh took care of her. When she got better, she stayed with the Guru as one of his bodyguards. After the Guru died, she retired and lived to an old age.

Her house has been made into a gurdwara. It is named after her. Mai Bhago shows that men and women are equal in Sikhism.

► *Mai Bhago in battle*

The Sahibzadas

This is the name that was given to the sons of Guru Gobind Singh. His 2 older sons were killed in battle. This is the story of the death of the younger boys.

The emperor told all Sikhs to leave Anandpur. The 2 boys left the fort with their grandmother. They stayed at the home of one of the Guru's servants, but he stole their gold. When the grandmother asked him about the gold, he was angry. He went to the authorities and told them that the Guru's family was hiding in his house. They sent police and arrested them. The servant was given a large sum of money as a reward.

The Guru's sons were taken before the ruler. They impressed everyone by their lack of fear and devotion to God.

The ruler promised them anything they wanted if they gave up their religion. They said:

> We don't care for worldly wealth. Nothing will make us give up our religion.

The boys should have been released. They had committed no crime and they were only children. But they told the ruler that they would fight until his rule was ended. At this point the order was given that they should be bricked up alive. The ruler insisted that the boys die, even though many people said it was wrong to do so.

◀ *The 2 boys are arrested with their grandmother*

The sentence was carried out. Two other prisoners were freed for doing this terrible deed. The boys were given another chance to give up their religion. Again they replied:

> We shall never give up our faith . . . Death has no meaning for us.

A wall was built around the 2 boys, but still they refused to give up their faith. When the boys became unconscious, it upset those building the wall. They pulled it down, dragged out the unconscious boys, and killed them. Their elderly grandmother died before hearing about it.

These are just 2 of the martyrs of the Sikh religion. Nothing could shake their faith. This encourages Sikhs, even today, to be brave and strong in their faith.

A Hindu poet wrote:

> ... the future of a community whose sons can lay down their lives for their faith is bound to be glorious.

Key words

martyr
Sahibzadas

► *The wall is built around the Sahibzadas who show no fear*

1. In pairs, read the story of Mai Bhago again. Decide on the FOUR most important events in the story. Divide a page into FOUR parts. Draw a picture of these FOUR events. Write a brief explanation underneath each picture.
2. Do the same for the story of the Guru's sons.
3. Think about the qualities that Mai Bhago and the Sahibzadas showed. Try to list SIX words or phrases to describe them.

Maharaja Ranjit Singh

Sikhs suffered for another 100 years after the death of Guru Gobind Singh. But at the end of the 18th century, the Sikh armies gained the upper hand. In 1799 the city of Lahore fell to a 19-year-old general named Ranjit Singh. He was a very brave soldier. **He was called the Lion of the Punjab. He made Lahore the capital of an empire that covered the Punjab. He became the Maharaja, which means 'great king'. He ruled until his death in 1839 when the British took over.**

During his reign many gurdwaras were repaired or built. He visited the Golden Temple of Amritsar and washed in the tank of water. He set up a council to run the Golden Temple. He did a lot of work on the building. He put the golden roof on it and gold work inside. He provided beautiful marble and paintings for it and a hall of mirrors. He built the silver-covered gate at the entrance to the bridge across the tank.

His rule was a time of peace. He was fair to everyone, whatever religion they followed. There were Muslims and Hindus in his army, as well as Sikhs. His ministers included Hindus, Muslims, Britons and Americans, as well as Sikhs.

Maharaja Ranjit Singh was a great man. Yet he lived a simple life. He is remembered for the fairness with which he treated all people. He shows what good can be done when Sikh beliefs are used to rule a country.

▲ *Maharaja Ranjit Singh*

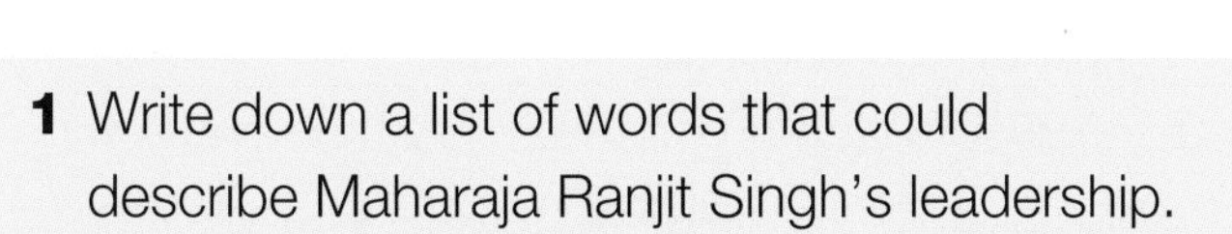

1 Write down a list of words that could describe Maharaja Ranjit Singh's leadership.

2 Maharaja Ranjit Singh was only 12 when he became leader, and 19 when he won a great victory. Discuss:

a) What responsibilities do most 12 year olds have in our society today?

b) Do you think adults sometimes underestimate what young people can do? Can you think of any examples?

Bhagat Puran Singh

> There can be no love of God without active service.
>
> *Guru Nanak*

Bhagat Puran Singh was born in 1904 near Lahore. He came from a poor family and had little education. He spent his life helping those in need. He was born a Hindu, but he became a Sikh. He helped out at a gurdwara in Lahore. At the age of 19 he vowed never to marry. Instead, he gave all of his time to the needy. He made the streets of Lahore safe by clearing the rubble. He made sure that those who died with no family were properly cremated.

In 1934 he found a crippled child. For many years he cared for the boy. He carried him around on his back, like any loving parent. When the boy grew too big, he had a cart made for him.

▼ *Bhagat Puran Singh spent his life in the service of others*

In 1947 he began the Pingalwara, or Home for the Handicapped. It started with just a few tents to care for the sick and dying. Today they have proper buildings. It is now supported by the main Sikh council, the SGPC. There are also collection boxes for it in towns and cities across the Punjab. Sikhs throughout the world raise money to support this work.

In 1991 Bhagat Puran Singh's name was put forward for the Nobel Peace Prize. **He was called the Mother Teresa of the Punjab and the Bearded saint of Amritsar. He died in 1992, but his work goes on**. The SGPC set up a special award for social service in his name. He was a great man. He set an example to Sikhs of the importance of service to others.

A famous Sikh writer said of him:

> He had nothing except his single-minded dedication to serve the poor and needy. And yet he was able to help thousands of lepers, the mentally and physically disabled people and the dying.

1 Bhagat Puran Singh loved learning, but he was too poor to have a proper education. Discuss:
a) How do you think your life might have been different if you had left school at 11?
b) What do you hope to do with your education?

2 Why was Bhagat Puran Singh called the Mother Teresa of the Punjab?

3 In pairs, divide a page into TWO columns: on one side, make a list of people's needs, on the other side, write down what you could do about that need. Discuss your ideas with the class.

Sant Jarnail Singh Bhindranwhale

▲ *Sant Jarnail Singh Bhindranwhale*

TASK

Heroes are people you look up to and want to be like.

- What heroes does the class have and why?
- What difference have they made to your lives?

Sant Jarnail Singh Bhindranwhale was born in 1947 and became a preacher. He was very strict about his religion. He was called Sant, which means saintly.

He became well known in the late 1970s when things got very bad for Sikhs under Indian rule. He and his followers went to the Golden Temple of Amritsar for safety. The Indian army attacked the Golden Temple on 1 June 1984. The Sikhs fought back. The firing finally stopped on 6 June. By this time the building called the Akal Takht was nearly destroyed and the Golden Temple was badly damaged. Nearly 1200 people were killed in that short time. Among the dead was Sant Jarnail Singh Bhindranwhale. He became a Sikh hero.

His death and the attack on this holy place shocked Sikhs all over the world. He was very popular with young people. Since his death, many young Sikhs have turned to their religion again.

▲ *This shows the damage to the Akal Takht, and what it looks like today*

1 Choose ONE of the 3 great Sikhs from this chapter. Design a poster to show his greatness.

17 Equality and the Place of Women

There is no difference between a temple and a mosque,
nor between the prayers of a Hindu or a Muslim.
Though differences seem to mark them out, all people are really the same ...
With eyes the same, the ears and body, all having a common form,
all are in fact a single creation, the parts of nature in one blend ...
All are the same, none is separate; a single form, a single creation.

Guru Gobind Singh

▲ *All Sikhs sit at the same level on the floor in the gurdwara. This shows they are equal*

Equality is very important in Sikhism. Sikhs believe that they should treat everyone the same. It doesn't matter about class, colour, race, religion or gender (male or female).

Equality can be seen in many of the things that Sikhs do:

- They sit at the same level in the gurdwara.
- Both men and women can lead the worship.
- The holy book has hymns by Hindus and Muslims as well as the Sikh Gurus.
- They share Karah Parshad together.
- They eat together in the langar.

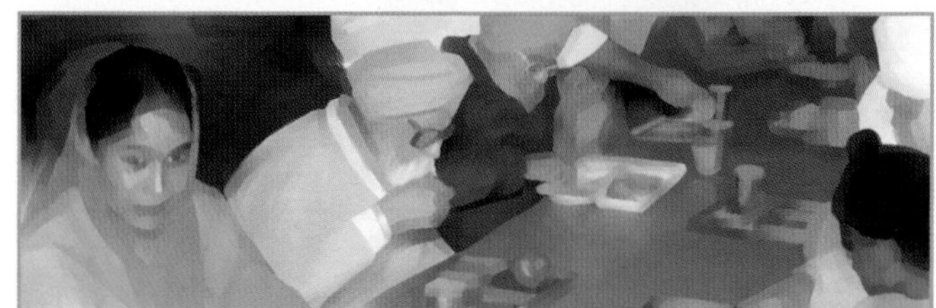

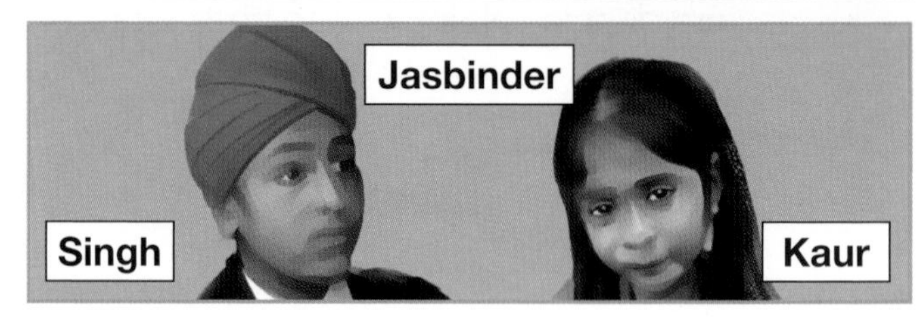

▲ *Some of the ways in which people are treated equally in Sikhism*

Men and women are treated the same from birth. First names can be the same for boys and girls. The only difference is that girls add the name Kaur, and boys add the name Singh. Members of the Khalsa must wear the Five Ks, whether they are men or women.

Here is what some Sikhs say about equality:

- There's only one thing better than any other – that's God. Everybody else is equal. That's what the Gurus said.
- There's no difference between men and women in religion. Any differences are because of the old way of living.
- There are no limits in the religious sense on women. Among Sikhs, women have equal rights to men. They can perform important ceremonies and do any work or service a man can do.

The Place of Women

The Gurus did a lot to improve the status of women. Guru Nanak said:

> It is by woman that we are conceived,
> And from her that we are born; it is with her that we are betrothed and married.
> It is woman we befriend, it is she who keeps the race going.
> When one woman dies, we seek another; it is with her we become established in society.
> Why should we call her inferior, who gives birth to great men?

Guru Nanak said this more than 450 years ago. Yet the Sex Discrimination Act only became law in England in 1975. Sikhism has always given women equal rights. They can do any work that a man can.

The Sikh code of conduct says this:

> A Sikh should respect another man's wife as he would his own mother; and another man's daughter as he would his own daughter.
>
> *Rahit*

Sikhism also protects women. It does not allow child marriage. This was common in India in Guru Nanak's day. Some Hindu widows burnt to death on their husband's funeral pyres. This was also forbidden in Sikhism, and widows could remarry.

▲ *Here is a woman reading the Guru Granth Sahib in the gurdwara*

1 In small groups, design a poster showing how Sikhism treats everyone the same.

2 Sikh boys and girls can be given the same name. In pairs, make a list of other names you can think of which can be given to both boys and girls. (They may be spelt differently, eg Lesley (girl) and Leslie (boy).)

3 Do you think men and women should be able to do the same jobs?

a) Is there any job that you think women shouldn't do? Give your reasons.

b) Is there any job that you think men shouldn't do? Give your reasons.

18 Past, Present and Future

▲ *Special dress shows that they are Sikhs*

> **TASK**
>
> Talk about anything in the news at the moment which has shocked you because of the way people have been treated.
>
> - List some examples.
> - How does it make you feel, when you hear news items like this?

In 1919 Sikhs gathered in Amritsar for the celebration of Vaisakhi. The British army entered the area and opened fire. It was not a political meeting. There wasn't a riot. These people were mainly peaceful family groups. Hundreds were killed or injured.

The whole of India was shocked. It made Sikhs very angry. They wanted to manage their own religion. In 1920 they set up a committee to manage all the gurdwaras. In 1925 they were given the right, by law, to control all those in the Punjab.

> Blessed is the death of martyrs,
> Should they meet death in a worthy cause.
>
> *Guru Nanak*

Britain gave India independence in 1947. At the same time, a separate Muslim country was set up. It was called Pakistan. It was later split into Pakistan and Bangladesh. **Sikhs also wanted their own state, called Khalistan. But they were ignored. The Punjab was split between Pakistan and India.** This made more than 2,000,000 Sikhs homeless.

▲ *A poster showing Sikh support for the idea of Khalistan*

After 1966, Sikhs did begin to have more of a say in India. But things went badly wrong again in June 1984. This was when the Indian army attacked the Sikhs at the Golden Temple. Sikhs everywhere were shocked:

> I realised I was a Sikh . . . it was me they were doing this to . . . but I wasn't doing anything about my religion. That's why I wear the Five Ks and a turban. It's good to find your real self.

The Indian prime minister was Mrs Indira Gandhi. Later that year, on 31 October 1984, she was killed by 2 of her Sikh bodyguards. Terrible violence broke out against Sikhs. Many innocent people were killed. The violence has never really finished since that time.

Sikhs live all over the world, but the Punjab is their homeland. These events have made Sikhs all over the world think about their religion. Many more young Sikhs are joining the Khalsa and wearing the Five Ks. They are less interested in all the things society offers.

Sikhs are calling again for a separate Sikh nation called Khalistan. Sikhs in the north of India are willing to die for this cause. They want to follow the example set by martyrs like Sant Jarnail Singh Bhindranwhale.

Like them, they want to be saint-soldiers. They are ready to lay down their lives in the service of others and their religion.

> Let my mind be guided only to ... sing Your praises,
> And when the time comes, I should die fighting bravely in battle.
>
> *Dasam Granth*
> *the favourite prayer of Guru Gobind Singh*

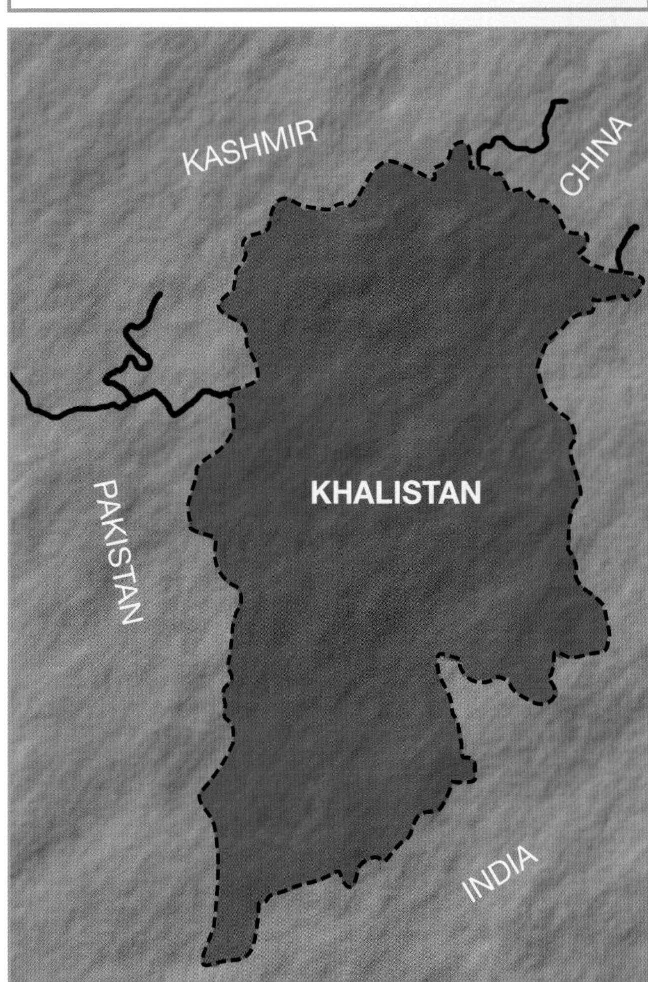

► *A map showing where the state of Khalistan might be located*

1 Find all the events in this chapter that have been given a date. Draw a time-line and put on it the events listed in this chapter.

2 What is Khalistan?

3 a) In groups, cut out pictures from colour magazines and make a collage to show the things that society offers young people (eg large homes, fast cars).
b) What are the things which tempt you most?
c) Why do you think many young Sikhs are no longer interested in these things?

Sikh Culture in a New Millennium

Sikhs in the entertainment industry influence life in India and other parts of the world.

Films

The Indian film industry is based in Mumbai (Bombay). It is known as Bollywood (after the American 'Hollywood'). Many of the most famous film directors are from the Punjab. Sikhs are very important to the Indian film industry.

The stories in Indian films are mostly about courtship and marriage. Some recent films have tackled more sensitive subjects. For instance, there was a film on the life of Guru Gobind Singh. The Guru himself was never shown in the film, although his story was told. This was because Sikhs would have been offended if someone had acted as the Guru.

Dancing

Bhangra dancing is popular among Sikhs. The dancers, like those in the photo, dress in colourful costumes. They wear head-dresses and waistcoats. They tie bells to their ankles.

It is based on a folk-dance which the men used to do at the harvest. They mime things like cutting the crop. They dance to the beat of the drums. Often they twirl full-length swords, while other dancers jump over them (but sometimes they use scarves). They shout encouragement to each other as the dance speeds up. Bhangra dancing is very energetic. The dancers have to be very fit. It was seen as good practice for battle.

Women sometimes join in with bhangra dancing today. But they also have a similar dance of their own.

▶ *Bhangra dancing*

Music

Punjabi pop music is also important. This, too, is called bhangra. It has a very strong beat. It became popular in the 1960s with groups like A S Kang and Alaap. Alaap used modern Western instruments along with the Indian ones. The more modern styles use either reggae or rap to make it different.

The first singer using bhangra to have a big hit outside India was Apache Indian. He is not an American Indian, despite the name, but comes from the Punjab. He combined bhangra and reggae music.

There are many other popular Asian singers. Malkit Singh is a Sikh from the Punjab. He and his group are very well known for their bhangra music. He was originally with the group Golden Star. He has made many hit records and has toured Canada, USA and India. He has made a record with Apache Indian for the UK pop music market.

▲ *Malkit Singh*

Malkit Singh said in an interview:

> I have immense faith in God. It is with His help that I've got where I am today. Being a Sikh, I pray every morning. I pray especially before going on stage to do a show. So religion plays an important part in my life

In Britain there are many Asian pop groups whose members are Sikhs. One example is the lead singer of the popular band Safri Boyz from Birmingham.

▲ *Balwinder Safri of Safri Boyz*

1 a) What types of dancing do you like doing?
b) Why was bhangra dancing seen as good for soldiers?

2 a) How can you tell from the photos on this page that both of these pop singers are Sikhs?
b) Why do you think Malkit Singh prays before going on stage? How do you think it helps him?

3 What types of songs do you like? (If you have any tapes or CDs by Sikh singers, arrange with your teacher to bring them into school.)

20 Conclusion – Sikh Feelings and Thoughts

This chapter is made up of quotations. Those from the Guru Granth Sahib and the Dasam Granth (by Guru Gobind Singh) are in coloured blocks. The others, in boxes, are by Sikhs today.

These quotes sum up the important beliefs and ideas of Sikhism. They say how Sikhs feel about the world around them. They talk about the past, the present, and what they hope for in the future.

God, the World, People and the Guru Granth Sahib

Holy are the continents created by Thee;
Holy is Thy universe.
Holy are the worlds and all within them.
Guru Nanak

The fool is wrapped up in pleasures, which all result in suffering.
From pleasure comes the sin that people commit.
From pleasure comes the suffering and separation from God,
That destroys people spiritually.
Guru Nanak

By hearing the word
One learns of truth, contentment and is wise.
Guru Nanak

Truth is the remedy for all ills,
and washes away all sins.
Guru Nanak

Worship God and you get all you wish.
Worship others and waste your life.
Guru Amar Das

It is cruel to kill animals by force and call it sanctified food.
Kabir

- Whatever's good and bad in the world – God has created it. We can't hope to understand why. That's just how it is.
- Loving God is what we believe in. If you do, it's easy to care for others and see that everyone is important.
- The Guru Granth Sahib is the centre of all we believe and all we do. When you understand that, you can see why we give it such a special place in the gurdwara.

▲ *Young Sikhs leading worship in the gurdwara*

Worship

The purest of all religions is devotion to God's Name:
And pure actions.
The noblest of all acts
Is the removal of evil thoughts in the holy company.
The noblest of all efforts
Is constant meditation on God's Name.

Guru Arjan

So do the fallen become approved of in holy company.

Guru Ram Das

(NB '*holy company*' means the company of Sikhs.)

- Saying my prayers at the set time helps me. If things go wrong during the day I can see how unimportant they really are. If they go right I can say thank you to God for looking after me.
- It's important to go to the gurdwara and listen to the teaching from the holy book. Being with good people ... listening to the Guru's teachings helps me live my life better.

Festivals and Ceremonies

- We have new clothes at Vaisakhi and we go to the gurdwara. It's the coming of a new year. We go and pray as well when it's the Guru's birthday. We have an Akhand Path in the gurdwara. It goes on for 48 hours .
- When a child is given a name it is very special. They are given Amrit, the same mixture of sugar and water that is used when Sikhs join the Khalsa. Only the most faithful join the Khalsa. We hope our babies will be like that.
- Being married is holy. We try to work together and be as one – that is what God wants for us. By living like that we can get closer to God.

Death breaks all family ties, with parents and brothers, with wife and sons. All must be cut off by death. Guru Tegh Bahadur

▲ *Young Sikhs take an active part in modern life*

Personal Qualities and Behaviour

Violence, selfishness, greed and anger;
these are the four rivers of fire:
They consume whoever falls in;
Only those having God's grace can swim across.

Guru Nanak

He does not seek the rewards of this world . . .
He does not indulge in loose or selfish talk,
He hoards the wealth of forgiveness,
And burns away his desires by meditating on God.

Guru Nanak

Know all human beings to be stores of Divine Light:
Do not stop and ask about their class.

Guru Nanak

In order to deserve recognition in the world to come,
It is essential to give service in this world.

Guru Nanak

The true hero is the one who struggles
For the poor and the helpless.

Kabir

◀ *A Sikh girls' sports team*

1 In pairs, read what the Sikhs today have to say in this chapter.

a) What do they say on page 60 about the Guru Granth Sahib?

b) What do they say on page 61 about prayer (in the section on worship)?

c) What do they say about marriage (in the section on festivals and ceremonies)?

Glossary

Adi Granth – first collection of the writings of the Gurus
Akhand Path – non-stop reading of the Guru Granth Sahib
amrit – sugar-water
Amrit ceremony – when Sikhs join the Khalsa
Amritsar – 'pool of nectar' (ie sweet drink), centre of Sikhism

bhangra dancing – energetic folk-dance done mainly by Sikh men

Dasam Granth – collection of writings mainly by Guru Gobind Singh
Diwali – Indian festival of lights

Five Beloved Ones – first 5 men willing to lay down their lives for Guru Gobind Singh, those who represent them in ceremonies today
Five Ks – symbols worn by Khalsa Sikhs

Golden Temple – main Sikh gurdwara, in Amritsar
granthi – person who reads out the Guru Granth Sahib
gurdwara – 'door of the Guru', Sikh place of worship where the Guru Granth Sahib is kept
gurpurbs – 'Guru-days', festivals connected with the Gurus
guru – religious teacher
Guru – the 10 human leaders of Sikhism, and now the holy book
Guru Gobind Singh – the tenth Guru, the last human Guru
Guru Granth Sahib – Sikh holy book
Gurmukhi – a simple way of writing Punjabi, used in the Guru Granth Sahib
Guru Nanak – founder of Sikhism, the first Guru
Gutka – small collection of hymns taken from the Guru Granth Sahib

hukam – 'God's will', the holy book is opened at random and the first full hymn is read
hymn – religious song divided into verses

Ik Onkar – 'there is one God', Sikh symbol

kachha – shorts, one of the Five Ks
kangha – comb, one of the Five Ks
kara – bangle, one of the Five Ks
Karah Parshad – sweet food shared out at Sikh services
Kaur – 'princess', name given to Khalsa Sikh women
kesh – uncut hair, one of the Five Ks
Khalistan – name which would be given to a separate Sikh homeland in India
Khalsa – the community of baptised Sikhs
khanda – (1) the double-sided sword (2) the symbol for Sikhism
kirpan – sword, one of the Five Ks

langar – Sikh kitchen where free meals are served

martyr – someone who dies for their beliefs
miracle – amazing event that cannot be explained
'Mul Mantar' – prayer setting out the Sikh idea of God, written by Guru Nanak, at the beginning of the Guru Granth Sahib

Nishan Sahib – Sikh flag

Punjab – land where most Sikhs live

Rahit – code of conduct of the Khalsa
reincarnation – belief that we are reborn again and again
romala – beautiful coverings for the Guru Granth Sahib

Sikh – 'disciple/learner', name of follower of Sikhism
Sikhism – religion started by Guru Nanak
Singh – 'lion', name given to Khalsa Sikh men

takht – throne for the Guru Granth Sahib; centre of religious authority in Sikhism

Vaisakhi – Indian festival, when the Khalsa was started

Waheguru – 'Wonderful Lord'

Index